D1193630

HOMELAND SECURITY

HOMELAND SECURITY

Other books in the At Issue series:

HOMELAND SECURITY

James D. Torr, *Book Editor*

Daniel Leone, *President*
Bonnie Szumski, *Publisher*
Scott Barbour, *Managing Editor*
Helen Cothran, *Senior Editor*

GREENHAVEN
PRESS ®

San Diego • Detroit • New York • San Francisco • Cleveland
New Haven, Conn. • Waterville, Maine • London • Munich

For more information, contact
Greenhaven Press
27500 Drake Rd.
Farmington Hills, MI 48331-3535
Or you can visit our Internet site at http://www.gale.com

LIBRARY OF CONGRESS CATALOGING-IN-PUBLICATION DATA

Homeland security / James D. Torr, book editor.
    p. cm. — (At issue)
Includes bibliographical references and index.
ISBN 0-7377-2188-X (lib. : alk. paper) — ISBN 0-7377-2189-8 (pbk. : alk. paper)
    1. War on Terrorism, 2001– . 2. Terrorism—United States—Prevention.
3. Terrorism—Government policy—United States. 4. Civil rights—United States.
I. Torr, James D., 1974– . II. At issue (San Diego, Calif.)
HV6432.H66 2004
363.3'2'0973—dc21   2003054030

Printed in the United States of America

Contents

Introduction

"How much freedom are Americans willing to give up for safety from terrorists?" This question, posed by a January 2003 feature in *USA Today* newspaper, resides at the center of current debates about homeland security, debates that are proving long-lived. Indeed, more than a year after the September 11, 2001, terrorist attacks on America, the federal government's stepped-up homeland security efforts are still a major focus of public discourse.

New homeland security measures encompass a wide variety of efforts to prevent terrorist attacks. They include both specific policies, such as random baggage searches at airports, and broader policy changes in intelligence-gathering and law enforcement, such as the reforms that the FBI and CIA have instituted since September 11. Whatever their scope, homeland security measures are evaluated by both policymakers and outside observers using two major criteria: their effectiveness in preventing terrorist attacks and the impact they have on the American public.

Security versus freedom

Homeland security measures often involve striking a balance between greater safety and infringements on civil liberties, such as invasions of privacy, discrimination, and other curtailments of individual freedom. As *USA Today*'s Gene Stephens explains, "We cannot truly be free unless we have a reasonable degree of safety, but we cannot truly feel safe unless we are also secure from undue prying into our personal lives." Baggage searches at airports, for example, may deter potential hijackers, but they also invade the privacy of countless non-terrorists. Similarly, granting broader investigative powers to the FBI could help thwart future attacks but may also result in unwarranted government surveillance or harassment of many innocent people. Evaluating homeland security efforts thus becomes a question of trade-offs; security experts must decide to what degree civil liberties should be curtailed in order to strengthen homeland security.

While homeland security encompasses a vast array of efforts at the local, state, and national levels, three centerpieces of the federal government's homeland security strategy have been intelligence gathering, intelligence sharing, and immigration control. The Bush administration's efforts to improve the government's capabilities in each of these three areas have been among the most controversial issues surrounding homeland security.

Intelligence gathering

In the aftermath of September 11, a consensus quickly emerged that the tragedies were due in part to a breakdown in intelligence. Leaders from across the political spectrum questioned how al-Qaeda—a known terrorist network—had been able to plan and execute the September 11 attacks without attracting the attention of the CIA, the FBI, the National Security Agency (NSA), the Department of Defense, and other agencies charged with tracking terrorist threats. A key to preventing future attacks, it seemed, was to revitalize U.S. intelligence efforts.

To this end Congress passed, and President George W. Bush signed, the USA Patriot Act on October 26, 2001. The act gives new investigative powers to domestic law enforcement and international intelligence agencies. For example, it expands federal agents' power to conduct telephone and e-mail surveillance of suspected terrorists—measures that have alarmed some civil libertarians and privacy advocates.

Controversy over the PATRIOT Act highlights a fundamental theme in homeland security debates: In general Americans want the government to use its power to investigate and avert terrorist threats, but at the same time they oppose the idea of a "police state" in which the government continuously monitors average people. The challenge facing the government, according to William Webster, former FBI director and CIA chief, is "getting as much information as possible without impairing the rights of privacy that Americans have always considered dear. Everyone has a right to question, 'Why are they doing these things?'"

Intelligence sharing

Related to, but distinct from, the challenge of intelligence gathering is the issue of intelligence sharing. Critics of the government's counterterrorism measures have laid part of the blame for September 11 on a lack of communication between the FBI, CIA, and other federal agencies. According to this view, there were significant warning signs that, had they been heeded, could have averted the September 11 attacks. However, because of the compartmentalized nature of the U.S. intelligence apparatus, the various agencies charged with tracking terrorist threats were unable to recognize the warning signs because they were not communicating with one another. As former FBI agent David Major puts it, "If you don't share intelligence, you don't connect the dots."

To better connect the "dots"—the countless bits of information gathered through separate intelligence operations—Congress passed the Homeland Security Act, which became law on November 25, 2002. The act created a new cabinet-level agency, the Department of Homeland Security (DHS), to coordinate homeland security efforts. The DHS incorporates twenty-two federal agencies, including the Immigration and Naturalization Service, Coast Guard, and the Border Patrol—but not the FBI or CIA—and constitutes the biggest reorganization in the federal government since the Department of Defense was created in 1947. One of the primary roles of the DHS is to collect and coordinate intelligence from the FBI, CIA, NSA, and other agencies so that they can more easily recognize patterns and threats.

From a civil libertarian point of view, the problem with intelligence sharing—as with intelligence gathering—is its potential for abuse. By its very nature intelligence gathering—or more colloquially, spying—involves invasions of privacy that run counter to the Fourth Amendment's protection against unwarranted government searches. For this reason, spying has historically been justified as a tool of national security rather than law enforcement, to be used against foreign governments rather than U.S. citizens. Domestic law enforcement agencies, such as the FBI, who wish to conduct wiretaps or property searches in criminal investigations must obtain warrants and observe other rules of procedure that foreign intelligence agencies such as the CIA do not. The CIA, in turn, is prohibited from engaging in law enforcement or internal security functions. Many analysts worry that the DHS's emphasis on intelligence sharing may serve to remove the prohibitions on domestic spying and erode the regulatory framework that governs the use of sensitive information gained through intelligence operations.

Targeting immigrants

Many of the concerns over intelligence gathering and sharing, and homeland security measures in general, have to do with the how such measures might affect the general public, including immigrants. Indeed, the group of non-terrorists that has been most affected by homeland security measures is immigrants.

As a March 2003 report in the *Economist* notes:

> In the months after the September 11th attacks, some 1,200 immigrants, mostly Muslims, were rounded up by the police and immigration officials across the country. Some of these were held for months before seeing a lawyer or being brought before an immigration judge. Most have since been released, some were deported, and only a few were charged with a crime. This practice seems to have continued, though the government has stopped reporting arrests.

The PATRIOT Act authorizes the U.S. attorney general to detain noncitizens without a hearing or proof that they have committed a crime. The rationale behind these measures is easy to see: All nineteen of the September 11 hijackers were Muslim immigrants, and they are believed to have received help from other al-Qaeda operatives living in the United States. Nevertheless, the mass arrests, and particularly the secrecy and lack of judicial oversight that surrounded them, outraged many civil libertarians.

Moreover, homeland security measures targeted at immigrants go beyond the investigation of the September 11 attacks. Due to the fact that all nineteen of the September 11 hijackers entered the country legally with visas (although several of the hijackers' visas had expired), a major part of the government's homeland security effort is to more thoroughly screen visa applicants in the future and track visa-holders while they are in the United States. Immigration itself has become a homeland security issue, as evidenced by the transfer of immigration control duties to the DHS. Civil libertarians warn that the government's scrutiny of immigrants will lead to the harassment and investigation of Muslim Americans as well as Muslim immigrants.

Whether the topic is baggage checks at airports or the secret detainment of Arab immigrants, debates about homeland security often center on the balance between freedom and security. For many people, such as University of Chicago Law School professor Richard A. Posner, civil liberties should be curtailed in order to strengthen homeland security. He writes:

> If it is true . . . that the events of September 11 have revealed the United States to be in much greater jeopardy from international terrorism than had previously been believed . . . it stands to reason that our civil liberties will be curtailed. They *should* be curtailed, to the extent that the benefits in greater security outweigh the costs in reduced liberty. All that can be reasonably asked of the responsible legislative and judicial officials is that they weigh the costs as carefully as the benefits.

Taking the opposite view are civil libertarians such as the *Nation*'s legal affairs correspondent David Cole, who argues that overly strong homeland security measures pose a greater threat to freedom than terrorism does:

> It appears that the greatest threat to our freedoms is posed not by the terrorists themselves but by our own government's response. . . . Administration supporters argue that the magnitude of the new threat requires a new paradigm. But so far we have seen only a repetition of the old paradigm—broad incursions on liberties, largely targeted at unpopular noncitizens and minorities, in the name of fighting a war. What is new is that this war has no end in sight, and only a vaguely defined enemy, so its incursions are likely to be permanent.

The viewpoints in *At Issue: Homeland Security* examine the government's major homeland security measures, evaluating both their effectiveness and their social impact. The essays in this volume survey the views of politicians, military officials, law enforcement personnel, and constitutional scholars, who debate the best ways to ensure that America is both safe and free.

1

Homeland Security Measures Undermine Civil Liberties

American Civil Liberties Union

The ACLU is a national organization that defends Americans' civil rights as guaranteed in the U.S. Constitution.

Since the September 11, 2001, terrorist attacks on America, the federal government has exercised new and unnecessary powers that severely undermine civil liberties. Federal authorities have jailed more than one thousand immigrant noncitizens without providing justification for their detention, and the USA PATRIOT Act and other laws have granted broad new surveillance powers to the FBI, CIA, and other agencies, which are being used to invade the privacy of citizens and noncitizens alike. Worst of all, an air of secrecy permeates much of the government's homeland security measures. The federal grab for new and overly broad powers, performed in the name of homeland security, threatens to erode the fundamental American ideals of liberty and open government.

Public Law 107-56 bears an extravagant title: The Uniting and Strengthening America by Providing Appropriate Tools Required to Intercept and Obstruct Terrorism Act. Its acronym—the USA PATRIOT Act—seems calculated to intimidate.

Indeed, the legislative process preceding the law's enactment featured both rhetoric and procedures designed to stifle voices of opposition. Soon after the tragic September 11 [2001] terrorist attacks, Attorney General John Ashcroft transmitted to Congress a proposal containing the Justice Department's wish list of new police powers, including dramatic new authority to obtain sensitive private information about individuals, eavesdrop on conversations, monitor computer use and detain suspects without probable cause, all with diminished judicial oversight. Ashcroft demanded that his proposal be enacted within three days, and, when that

American Civil Liberties Union, *Insatiable Appetite: The Government's Demand for New and Unnecessary Powers After September 11*, April 2002. Copyright © 2002 by American Civil Liberties Union. Reproduced by permission.

deadline was not met, he suggested publicly that members of Congress would be responsible for any terrorist attack that occurred during the bill's pendency. Congress passed the far-reaching law after abbreviated debate, handing Ashcroft virtually all the investigative tools he sought and several he had not even asked for.

Yet the Government's hunger for new powers was not satisfied. Soon after passage of the USA PATRIOT Act, Justice Department spokeswoman Mindy Tucker declared: "This is just the first step. There will be additional items to come."

Additional items have come, some in the form of peremptory executive actions. Officials have detained hundreds of Middle Eastern and South Asian men and engaged in dragnet questioning of thousands of others without individualized suspicion. The Administration has asserted unilateral authority to establish secret military tribunals and breach attorney-client communications without a court order. It has even locked up American citizens in military brigs without charging them with a crime and has argued they should have no access to the courts. When challenged, government officials insist their actions represent a natural reordering of the balance between liberty and security. But while the loss of liberty is apparent, there is surprisingly little evidence that the new powers will actually enhance security.

Government policies should not be based on the myth that liberties must be curtailed to protect the public.

The loss of liberty associated with these new measures takes various forms, but can be distilled into three basic overarching themes:

- An unprecedented and alarming new penchant for government secrecy and abandonment of the core American principle that a government for the people and by the people must be transparent to the people.
- A disdain for the checks and balances that have been a cornerstone of American democracy for more than 225 years. Specifically, the Administration has frequently bypassed Congress, while both the Executive and Legislative branches have weakened the Judiciary's authority to check government excesses.
- A disrespect for the American value of equality under the law. Government enforcement strategies that target suspects based on their country of origin, race, religion or ethnicity pose a serious threat to the civil liberties of citizens and non-citizens alike. . . .

Working with other organizations, the ACLU [American Civil Liberties Union] has also brought its arguments to the courts, filing lawsuits to uncover information about hundreds of detainees, challenge a new law prohibiting non-citizens from working as airport screeners and obtain public access to immigration hearings. The ACLU continues to insist that the dichotomy between security and liberty is false: we believe that we can be both safe *and* free, and that government policies should not be based on the myth that liberties must be curtailed to protect the public. . . .

Some of the new statutes, rules and executive orders adopted in the [year following the September 11 attacks] may be benign while others are obviously troublesome. But in any event there has been little showing that the post 9-11 avalanche of laws, in the aggregate, make America safer. And, while the benefit of these measures is hard to discern, *there is no question* that they exact a profound cost to civil liberties and core constitutional values.

Would efforts to prevent terrorism be any less successful if in the weeks after the attacks Congress had merely appropriated funds for existing agencies, authorized the deployment of troops to Afghanistan,[1] and if the executive branch had simply exercised its extant pre-September 11 powers?

The threat to patriotic dissent

Looming over other threats is the threat that those who voice opposition to government policies will be branded unpatriotic. The most basic of all American values, one that buttresses all others, is the First Amendment right to express dissenting views about government actions.

Attorney General Ashcroft has a different view. Testifying before the Senate Judiciary Committee on December 6, 2001, the Attorney General stated, in his prepared remarks, "To those who scare peace-loving people with phantoms of lost liberty, my message is this: Your tactics only aid terrorists, for they erode our national unity and diminish our resolve. They give ammunition to America's enemies and pause to America's friends."

This threat, though chilling, was hollow. If the Attorney General hoped to silence critics of the Administration's anti-terror tactics he has plainly failed, because public concern about those tactics is growing, not waning.

Yet it appears that the Attorney General's sentiment has been translated into action. Reports have emerged recently of federal agents investigating an art museum that exhibited materials on American covert operations and government secrets, a student who displayed a poster critical of President [George W.] Bush's position on the death penalty and a San Francisco weightlifter who publicly criticized the Administration, among others.

The threat to liberty

Individual liberty is the central precept of our system of government, but new government powers challenge that value in both extreme and subtle ways.

One of the most significant attacks on individual liberty in the name of anti-terrorism is the government's lengthy detention of individuals whose conduct has not warranted such a deprivation. At one time more than a thousand individuals were jailed in reaction to September 11. Today that number is smaller, but the Justice Department still refuses to provide a precise accounting. Some may deserve to be detained for criminal conduct, but many do not.

Conservative columnist Stuart Taylor, who has defended a number of the new anti-terror measures, observes that:

1. The United States sent troops to Afghanistan in 2001 to fight the Taliban, the ruling regime that harbored al-Qaeda, the terrorist network responsible for the September 11 attacks.

Not since the World War II internment of Japanese-Americans have we locked up so many people for so long with so little explanation. The same logic that made it prudent to err on the side of overinclusiveness in rounding up suspects after the crimes of September 11 makes it imperative to ensure that these people are treated with consideration and respect, that they have every opportunity to establish their innocence and win release, and that they do not disappear for weeks or months into our vast prison-jail complex without explanation.

A more long-term infringement of liberty is posed by the loss of privacy that will result from many of the provisions in the USA PATRIOT Act and related measures. The new authorities interfere with the right to privacy by making it easier for the government to conduct surveillance, listen in on conversations, obtain sensitive financial, student and medical records and otherwise track the daily activities of individuals. Subjecting individuals to intrusive police questioning without particularized suspicion is an additional deprivation of liberty that has flourished in recent months. The potential for such deprivation increased with the decision to allow the CIA to, once again, compile dossiers on ordinary Americans and then—through new information sharing provisions—distribute that information throughout the law enforcement and intelligence communities.

Not since the World War II internment of Japanese-Americans have we locked up so many people for so long with so little explanation.

Defenders of liberty do not take issue with the minor inconveniences that accompany many current security measures. Few Americans quarrel, for example, with reasonable screening procedures in airports such as luggage matching and strict control of secure areas to prevent weapons from being carried onto airplanes. Rather, the debate is about measures, like the USA PATRIOT Act, that represent genuine encroachments on privacy. Opinion polls suggest that a growing number of Americans are unwilling to sacrifice core values in the fight against terrorism, especially without proof that any particular measure is likely to be effective.

Before it may scrutinize such personally sensitive materials as medical records, school records, banking records or an individual's Internet use, the government should be required to demonstrate in a particularized fashion that such scrutiny is necessary to achieve safety. That balance, of course, is embodied in the Fourth Amendment, which prohibits "unreasonable" searches and seizures and authorizes the government to intrude on privacy only upon a finding of probable cause by a neutral judge.

The new enforcement powers conferred by Congress and assumed by the Justice Department reflect impatience with the Fourth Amendment, and its embodiment of the fundamental American conviction that individual liberty is accorded the benefit of the doubt when enforcing criminal law. The surveillance authorities in the USA PATRIOT Act undermine the role of the courts as the protectors of the individual against unfair and unwarranted government scrutiny or harassment. And the new Ashcroft surveillance guidelines reflect the view that dissent is to be feared and monitored, not protected under the First Amendment.

The threat to equality

The Constitution guarantees equal protection of the laws. It prohibits the government from establishing different sets of rules for similarly situated groups without a compelling reason. Citizenship is a characteristic upon which some distinctions may be made, but not others. For example, non-citizens may not vote in federal elections but they are entitled to equal treatment, due process and other constitutional protections by virtue of their presence in the country.

It is striking how many of the new restrictions and investigative tactics distinguish between citizens and non-citizens. Many of the government's actions, such as the military tribunal framework, the dragnet interviews and of course the immigration-related detentions, all apply to non-citizens but not citizens. Also, new rules prohibit non-citizens from serving as airline screeners and limit the jobs non-citizens may perform at certain federal facilities.

The broad premise of this distinction is that non-citizens pose a threat to Americans that citizens do not. That the 19 men who hijacked planes [on September 11] were non-citizens makes this premise superficially appealing, but in fact citizenship is a highly unreliable proxy for evidence of dangerousness.

First, at least one of the Al Qaeda [terrorist network] members convicted in the trial arising from the terror attack on U.S. embassies in Africa was an American citizen (Wadih el-Hage), and at least two American citizens have been apprehended as suspected Taliban soldiers (John Walker Lindh and Yaser Esam Hamdi). Second, the President has made clear that the war on terrorism is not limited to Al Qaeda and the Taliban but encompasses all who utilize violence to intimidate civilian populations. By that measure, there have been numerous U.S. citizen-terrorists, including Timothy McVeigh whose bombing of the federal building in Oklahoma City was the bloodiest act of terrorism on U.S. soil prior to September 11.

An undue investigative focus on non-citizens threatens to spill over into . . . harassment of citizens who happen to "look foreign" or who have "foreign-sounding" names.

But while some citizens are terrorists, a more important fact is that the overwhelming majority of non-citizens are not terrorists. Of the millions of non-citizens residing in the United States legally or illegally, only an infinitesimally small number of them have been tied to September 11 or other terror plots. As a statistical matter, citizenship status reveals essentially nothing about likely involvement in terrorism. Factoring in age and gender by focusing on young male non-citizens does not meaningfully narrow the targeted class.

The pattern of detentions, the efforts to selectively deport out-of-status non-citizens and the dragnet effort to question 8,000 young Arab and South Asian men and fingerprint 100,000 more constitute profiling on the basis of national origin. Profiling is a flawed law enforcement tactic and a flawed tactic in the war on terrorism. It is inefficient and ineffective, since it squanders limited law enforcement resources based on a factor that bears no statistically significant relationship to wrongdoing. Also, unwarranted focus on non-citizens as a class engenders hostility and resentment in immigrant communities. Yet it is precisely those communities in which law enforcement agencies are now seeking to recruit agents, hire translators and search for suspicious behavior.

> *The Administration's [Freedom of Information Act] policies threaten to usher in a new era of government secrecy.*

An undue investigative focus on non-citizens threatens to spill over into governmental or non-governmental harassment of citizens who happen to "look foreign" or who have "foreign-sounding" names. Already the federal government's reliance on a national origin dragnet has spawned similar tactics: detectives in New York City's warrant squad have prioritized their activities by culling through computers for petty crime suspects with Middle Eastern-sounding names. And on more than 200 college campuses investigators have contacted administrators to collect information about students from Middle Eastern countries and have approached foreign students without notice to conduct "voluntary" interviews.

Reliance on mere non-citizenship as a distinguishing characteristic is not just ineffective law enforcement; it is also anathema to American values. Vice President [Dick] Cheney has said that those who kill innocent Americans would get "the kind of treatment we believe they deserve" since such people do not deserve "the same guarantees and safeguards that would be used for an American citizen going through the normal judicial process." The Vice President's dichotomy between "an American citizen" and "those who kill innocent Americans" is dangerously misleading. Citizenship is simply not a trait that distinguishes those who kill innocent Americans from those who do not.

The threat to constitutional checks and balances

The Administration's actions since enactment of the USA PATRIOT Act betray a serious disrespect for the role of Congress. That law emerged from a flawed legislative process, and a number of the subsequently announced initiatives were never even discussed with Congress. For example, painstaking negotiations with Congress over the circumstances under which non-citizens could be detained in the name of national security led to enactment of section 412 of the Act, which limits detentions to seven days before the individual must be brought before a judge to face immigration or criminal charges. But just after enactment, the Administration unveiled its military tribunal proposal, permitting indefinite detention of non-citizens without any review by an independent judicial officer. Now the designation of certain individuals as "enemy combatants" renders even the meager protections of the military tribunal regulations inoperative.

Moreover, both the USA PATRIOT Act and the subsequent executive actions undermine the role of the judiciary in overseeing the exercise of executive authority. The Act essentially codifies a series of short cuts for government agents. Under many of its provisions, a judge exercises no review function whatsoever; the court must issue an order granting access to sensitive information upon mere certification by a government official. The Act reflects a distrust of the judiciary as an independent safeguard against abuse of executive authority.

This trend is particularly apparent in the electronic surveillance provisions of the Act. For example, the USA PATRIOT Act subjects surveillance of Internet communications to a minimal standard of review. This surveillance would reveal the persons with whom one corresponded by e-mail and the websites one visited. Law enforcement agents may access this information by merely certifying that the information is relevant to an ongoing investigation. The court must accept the law enforcement certification; the judge must issue the order even if he or she finds the certification factually unpersuasive.

The subsequent executive actions are even more flawed in this regard. The regulation allowing for monitoring of attorney-client communications was promulgated to bypass the courts, since prior to its promulgation government agents could only engage in such monitoring if they obtained a court-issued warrant and now they may act upon their own suspicions without judicial review. And the military tribunal order and military detention of American citizens constitute pure court-stripping by removing federal judges from the process altogether.

These initiatives misunderstand the role of the judiciary in our constitutional system. They treat the courts as an inconvenient obstacle to executive action rather than an essential instrument of accountability.

The Framers of the Constitution understood that legislative and judicial checks on executive authority are important bulwarks against abusive government. It is true that the President plays a heightened role as Commander in Chief in defending the nation against foreign threats. But current circumstances do not render ordinary constitutional constraints on his role inoperative or unnecessary.

The threat to open government

In our democracy, executive and legislative actions derive legitimacy from the fact that they emerge from a process that is deliberative and largely open to the public, at least through the media. But many of the new anti-terrorism measures fail this fundamental test.

As described above, much of the USA PATRIOT Act was negotiated out of public view. Key stages of the legislative process—commitee vote, floor debate, and conference—were either short-circuited or skipped altogether. Similarly, the executive order concerning attorney-client communications and the presidential order authorizing military tribunals were developed in secret with no opportunity for public debate about their efficacy or wisdom before their promulgation.

At the same time, secrecy permeates the process by which hundreds of young Arab and South Asian men have been detained by the government. One reason the justice system must be open to the public is to ensure that the government affords individuals due process consistent with the Constitution and applicable statutes. One detainee was held for eight months without being brought before a judge. Georgetown Law Professor David Cole has observed: "In open proceedings the government would never get away with holding a person for three weeks without bringing charges. The only reason they have gotten away with it is these proceedings have been conducted under a veil of secrecy."

The Administration's FOIA [Freedom of Information Act] policies threaten to usher in a new era of government secrecy. While the Attorney General invoked the threat to terrorism in his directive limiting FOIA compliance, the order covers all government information, much of which has no national security or law enforcement connection whatsoever. As a result, all executive branch activities will be less open and less accountable under this new regime.

To be sure, there is a need for some secrecy in times of crisis. No one advocates the disclosure of documents that might endanger troops on the battlefield. But secrecy appears to be a hallmark of the Bush Administration's every move, even in the development of policies that should emerge from the crucible of public scrutiny and in the adjudication of charges against individuals.

The threat to the rule of law

It is often said that ours is a government of laws, not those who inhabit high office at any given moment. Americans may trust or admire such individuals, but their enduring faith is reserved for certain fundamental legal principles and traditions that emanate from our Constitution: that the federal government is one of limited, enumerated powers; that the Congress makes the law, the President executes the law, and the judiciary interprets the law; that criminal suspects are innocent until proven guilty and entitled to various procedural protections during the process of adjudicating guilt. Many of the new powers assumed by the President and his officers since September 11 run counter to these principles.

For example, the detention of Americans in military brigs, and the contemplated procedures for non-citizens facing military tribunals skirt the rule of law. Department of Defense guidelines governing the tribunals shows marked and alarming deviation from traditional courts martial.

First, while the Pentagon has codified tribunal procedures in a less offensive fashion than opponents originally feared, the tribunals still—unacceptably—lack a clear appeals process. The guidelines essentially give the final word on the accused's fate to the President or the Secretary of Defense.

Also, the guidelines confer complete discretion on the President or the Secretary of Defense to hold the tribunals in secrecy. Finally, in a surreal twist, it appears that the government will still be able to detain indefinitely suspects acquitted by the tribunals.

In the final analysis, the main difference between the tribunals and courts-martial is that nothing is binding with the tribunals. The Administration has given itself unlimited discretion to compose the rules for the tribunals as they go—an affront to the American tradition of impartial procedures to protect individual rights from the caprice of persons in authority.

American citizens are treated no better. According to the Bush Administration, the President need only sign an order labeling an American citizen an "enemy combatant" to begin a process in which the citizen can be held indefinitely—without charge and without a right to see a lawyer—until the "war on terrorism" has ended. And the Administration argues that no court can review the President's designation of an "enemy combatant."

America, more so than at any other time in the past three decades, stands at a crossroads.

Other facets of the war on terrorism also undermine the rule of law. Secret detentions, the unreviewable assertion of executive authority, the deployment of law enforcement agents against groups of people without particularized suspicion, recruiting ordinary Americans to spy on their neighbors—these are the hallmarks of undemocratic, strong-arm governments, not the two-century-old American democracy. Resorting to such tactics, even temporarily or in limited contexts, is cause for serious concern.

One reason for concern is that the new powers, especially many of the investigative tools in the USA PATRIOT Act, are not limited to the pursuit of terrorists. Even those that are reserved for terrorism investigations may be used in contexts that the drafters of the Act never contemplated. The label "terrorism" is notoriously elastic; it has recently come to light that the Department of Justice categorizes as "terrorism" such garden variety crimes as erratic behavior by people with mental illness, passengers getting drunk on airplanes, and convicts rioting to get better prison food.

In recent decades the United States has styled itself a champion of international human rights, and has encouraged the development of civilian legal institutions and the "rule of law" in countries throughout the world. For example, the State Department has pressured Egypt to abandon military tribunals in that country's war on terrorism, and has also criticized the secret trials that frequently characterize the justice systems in South America and China. What force will those criticisms have if the United States avails itself of these shortcuts even though its civilian courts are fully functional and open for business?

The need for vigilance

America, more so than at any time in the past three decades, stands at a crossroads. The Administration has invoked historical precedents to justify its wartime tactics, and in doing so has brought key segments of American society and politics to the brink of repeating much in our history that we have come to regret. It is true that throughout American history—from the 18th century Alien and Sedition Acts to the suspension of habeas corpus during the Civil War to the Palmer Raids and the internment of Japanese-Americans during World War II—constitutional protections have taken a back seat to national security. But with the benefit of hindsight, Americans have regretted such assertions of new government powers in times of crisis.

It is especially true that immigrants and others, citizens and non-citizens alike, have been mistreated in wartime. The disgraceful internment of Japanese-Americans remains a stain on our national honor. That is surely not a precedent on which the Administration would want to rely.

Concepts of due process, military justice and international human rights have advanced substantially since World War II. Departure from these principles has detrimental consequences for the war on terrorism. European allies, already wary of extraditing suspects to the United States because of opposition to the death penalty, have now expressed misgivings about the possibility of military tribunals and other measures.

Some national leaders downplay these concerns, saying that wartime limitations on civil liberties are temporary and normal conditions will return once hostilities end. But the war on terrorism, unlike conventional wars, is not likely to come to a public and decisive end. Both Homeland Security Director Tom Ridge and the newly appointed drug czar, John Walters, recently equated the war on terrorism with the nation's continuing wars on drugs and crime. So restrictions on civil liberties may be with us for a very long time. So long, in fact, that they may change the character of our democratic system in ways that very few Americans desire.

In the absence of a broader sunset provision in the USA PATRIOT Act, and since the subsequent orders and regulations are of indefinite duration, Congress must be vigilant in monitoring implementation of these new authorities. These powers have been structured in a manner that limits the role judges would ordinarily play in ensuring that enforcement agencies abide by constitutional and statutory rules. Without judicial oversight, there is a real danger that the war on terrorism will have domestic consequences that are inconsistent with American values and ideals.

It is as *New York Times* columnist Bob Herbert has written:

> We have a choice. We can fight and win a just war against terrorism, and emerge with the greatness of the United States intact. Or, we can win while running roughshod over the principles of fairness and due process that we claim to cherish, thus shaming ourselves in the eyes of the world—eventually, when the smoke of fear and anger finally clears—in our own eyes as well.

2

Homeland Security Measures Should Not Be Restricted by an Overly Broad View of Civil Liberties

Stuart Taylor Jr.

Stuart Taylor Jr. is a senior writer for National Journal.

Civil liberties have been curtailed in the wake of September 11, in some cases with little justification. But the claim of some civil libertarians that no curtailment of civil liberties is justified is simply false. Several law enforcement tactics that curtail civil liberties—including searches without a warrant, increased federal wiretapping and surveillance, coercive interrogation of suspects in custody, and detention of suspects who have not yet committed a crime—may be justified since they can help prevent terrorism. The responsible course of action is for legislators to determine what new governmental powers will improve homeland security and then set boundaries on these powers to prevent their overuse and abuse.

W hen dangers increase, liberties shrink. That has been our history, especially in wartime. And today we face dangers without precedent: a mass movement of militant Islamic terrorists who crave martyrdom, hide in shadows, are fanatically bent on slaughtering as many of us as possible and—if they can—using nuclear truck bombs to obliterate New York or Washington or both, without leaving a clue as to the source of the attack.

How can we avert catastrophe and hold down the number of lesser mass murders? Our best hope is to prevent al-Qaida[1] from getting nuclear, biological, or chemical weapons and smuggling them into this country.

---

1. Al-Qaeda is the terrorist network responsible for the September 11 attacks.

Stuart Taylor Jr., "Rights, Liberties, and Security: Recalibrating the Balance After September 11," *Brookings Review*, vol. 21, Winter 2003, pp. 25–31. Copyright © 2003 by The Brookings Institution. Reproduced by permission.

But we need be unlucky only once to fail in that. Ultimately we can hold down our casualties only by finding and locking up (or killing) as many as possible of the hundreds of thousands of possible al-Qaida terrorists whose strategy is to infiltrate our society and avoid attention until they strike.

The urgency of penetrating secret terrorist cells makes it imperative for Congress—and the nation—to undertake a candid, searching, and systematic reassessment of the civil liberties rules that restrict the government's core investigate and detention powers. Robust national debate and deliberate congressional action should replace what has so far been largely ad hoc presidential improvisation. While the USA-PATRIOT Act—no model of careful deliberation—changed many rules for the better (and some for the worse), it did not touch some others that should be changed.

Civil libertarians have underestimated the need for broader investigative powers and exaggerated the dangers to our fundamental liberties.

Carefully crafted new legislation would be good not only for security but also for liberty. Stubborn adherence to the civil liberties status quo would probably damage our most fundamental freedoms far more in the long run than would judicious modifications of rules that are less fundamental. Considered congressional action based on open national debate is more likely to be sensitive to civil liberties and to the Constitution's checks and balances than unilateral expansion of executive power. Courts are more likely to check executive excesses if Congress sets limits for them to enforce. Government agents are more likely to respect civil liberties if freed from rules that create unwarranted obstacles to doing their jobs. And preventing terrorist mass murders is the best way of avoiding a panicky stampede into truly oppressive police statism, in which measures now unthinkable could suddenly become unstoppable.

This is not to advocate truly radical revisions of civil liberties. Nor is it to applaud all the revisions that have already been made, some of which seem unwarranted and even dangerous. But unlike most in-depth commentaries on the liberty-security balance since September 11[2]—which argue (plausibly, on some issues) that we have gone too far in expanding government power—this article contends that in important respects we have not gone far enough. Civil libertarians have underestimated the need for broader investigative powers and exaggerated the dangers to our fundamental liberties. Judicious expansion of the government's powers to find suspected terrorists would be less dangerous to freedom than either risking possibly preventable attacks or resorting to incarceration without due process of law—as the Bush administration has begun to do. We should worry less about being wiretapped or searched or spied upon or interrogated and more about seeing innocent people put behind bars—or being blown to bits.

---

2. On September 11, 2001, terrorists flew planes into the World Trade Center in New York and the Pentagon in Washington, killing more than three thousand people.

Recalibrating the liberty-security balance

The courts, Congress, the president, and the public have from the beginning of this nation's history demarcated the scope of protected rights "by a weighing of competing interests . . . the public-safety interest and the liberty interest," in the words of Judge Richard A. Posner of the U.S. Court of Appeals for the Seventh Circuit. "The safer the nation feels, the more weight judges will be willing to give to the liberty interest."

During the 1960s and 1970s, the weight on the public safety side of the scales seemed relatively modest. The isolated acts of violence by groups like the Weather Underground and the Black Panthers—which had largely run their course by the mid-1970s—were a minor threat compared with our enemies today. Suicide bombers were virtually unheard of. By contrast, the threat to civil liberties posed by broad governmental investigative and detention powers and an imperial presidency had been dramatized by Watergate and by disclosures of such ugly abuses of power as FBI Director J. Edgar Hoover's spying on politicians, his wiretapping and harassment of the Reverend Martin Luther King, Jr., and the government's disruption and harassment of anti-war and radical groups.

To curb such abuses, the Supreme Court, Congress, and the Ford and Carter administrations placed tight limits on law-enforcement and intelligence agencies. The Court consolidated and in some ways extended the Warren Court's revolutionary restrictions on government powers to search, seize, wiretap, interrogate, and detain suspected criminals (and terrorists). It also barred warrantless wiretaps and searches of domestic radicals. Congress barred warrantless wiretaps and searches of suspected foreign spies and terrorists—a previously untrammeled presidential powers—in the 1978 Foreign Intelligence Surveillance Act. And Edward Levi, President [Gerald] Ford's attorney general, clamped down on domestic surveillance by the FBI.

As a result, today many of the investigative powers that government could use to penetrate al-Qaida cells—surveillance, informants, searches, seizures, wiretaps, arrests, interrogations, detentions—are tightly restricted by a web of laws, judicial precedents, and administrative rules. Stalked in our homeland by the deadliest terrorists in history, we are armed with investigative powers calibrated largely for dealing with drug dealers, bank robbers, burglars, and ordinary murderers. We are also stuck in habits of mind that have not yet fully processed how dangerous our world has become or how ill-prepared our legal regime is to meet the new dangers.

Rethinking government's powers

Only a handful of the standard law-enforcement investigative techniques have much chance of penetrating and defanging groups like al-Qaida. The four most promising are: infiltrating them through informants and undercover agents; finding them and learning their plans through surveillance, searches, and wiretapping; detaining them before they can launch terrorist attacks; and interrogating those detained. All but the first (infiltration) are now so tightly restricted by Supreme Court precedents (sometimes by mistaken or debatable readings of them), statutes, and administrative rules as to seriously impede terrorism investigators. Careful new legislation could make these powers more flexible and useful while simultaneously setting boundaries to minimize overuse and abuse.

Searches and surveillance

The Supreme Court's case law involving the Fourth Amendment's ban on "unreasonable searches and seizures" does not distinguish clearly between a routine search for stolen goods or marijuana and a preventive search for a bomb or a vial of anthrax. To search a dwelling, obtain a wiretap, or do a thorough search of a car or truck, the government must generally have "probable cause"—often (if incorrectly) interpreted in the more-probable-than-not sense—to believe that the proposed search will uncover evidence of crime. These rules make little sense when the purpose of the search is to prevent mass murder.

Federal agents and local police alike need more specific guidance than the Supreme Court can quickly supply. Congress should provide it, in the form of legislation relaxing for terrorism investigations the restrictions on searching, seizing, and wiretapping, including the undue stringency of the burden of proof to obtain a search warrant in a terrorism investigation.

Search and seizure restrictions were the main (if widely unrecognized) cause of the FBI's famous failure to seek a warrant during the weeks before September 11 to search the computer and other possessions of Zacarias Moussaoui, the alleged "20th hijacker." He had been locked up since August 16, [2002] technically for overstaying his visa, based on a tip about his strange behavior at a Minnesota flight school. The FBI had ample reason to suspect that Moussaoui—who has since admitted to being a member of al-Qaida—was a dangerous Islamic militant plotting airline terrorism.

Broader wiretapping authority is not all bad for civil liberties.

Congressional and journalistic investigations of the Moussaoui episode have focused on the intelligence agencies' failure to put together the Moussaoui evidence with other intelligence reports that should have alerted them that a broad plot to hijack airliners might be afoot. Investigators have virtually ignored the undue stringency of the legal restraints on the government's powers to investigate suspected terrorists. Until these are fixed, they will seriously hobble our intelligence agencies no matter how smart they are.

From the time of FDR [Franklin Delano Roosevelt] until 1978, the government could have searched Moussaoui's possessions without judicial permission, by invoking the president's inherent power to collect intelligence about foreign enemies. But the 1978 Foreign Intelligence Security Act (FISA) bars searches of suspected foreign spies and terrorists unless the attorney general can obtain a warrant from a special national security court (the FISA court). The warrant application has to show not only that the target is a foreign terrorist, but also that he is a member of some international terrorist "group."

Coleen Rowley, a lawyer in the FBI's Minneapolis office, argued passionately in a widely publicized letter [in May 2002] to FBI Director Robert S. Mueller III that the information about Moussaoui satisfied this FISA requirement. Congressional investigators have said the same. FBI headquarters officials have disagreed, because before September 11 no evidence linked Moussaoui to al-Qaida or any other identifiable terrorist group. Unlike their critics, the FBI headquarters officials were privy to any relevant prior decisions by the FISA court, which cloaks its proceedings and decisions in secrecy. In addition, they were understandably gun-shy about going forward with a legally shaky warrant application in the wake of the FISA court's excoriation of an FBI supervisor in the fall of 2000 for perceived improprieties in his warrant applications. In any event, even if the FBI had done everything right, it is at least debatable whether its information about Moussaoui was sufficient to support a FISA warrant.

More important for future cases, it is clear that FISA—even as amended by the USA-PATRIOT Act—will not authorize a warrant in any case in which the FBI cannot tie a suspected foreign terrorist to one or more confederates, whether because his confederates have escaped detection or cannot be identified or because the suspect is a lone wolf.

You do not have a right to remain silent.

Congress could strengthen the hand of FBI terrorism investigators by amending FISA to include the commonsense presumption that any foreign terrorist who comes to the United States is probably acting for (or at least inspired by) some international terrorist group. Another option would be to lower the burden of proof from "probable cause" to "reasonable suspicion." A third option—which could be extended to domestic as well as international terrorism investigations—would be to authorize a warrantless "preventive" search or wiretap of anyone the government has reasonable grounds to suspect of preparing or helping others prepare for a terrorist attack. To minimize any temptation for government agents to use this new power in pursuit of ordinary criminal suspects, Congress could prohibit the use in any prosecution unrelated to terrorism of any evidence obtained by such a preventive search or wiretap.

The Supreme Court seems likely to uphold any such statute as consistent with the ban on "unreasonable searches and seizures." While the Fourth Amendment says that "no warrants shall issue, but upon probable cause," warrants are not required for many types of searches, are issued for administrative searches of commercial property without probable cause in the traditional sense, and arguably should never be required. Even in the absence of a warrant or probable cause, the justices have upheld searches based on "reasonable suspicion" of criminal activities, including brief "stop-and-frisk" encounters on the streets and car stops. They have also upheld mandatory drug-testing of certain government employees and transportation workers whose work affects the public safety even when there is no particularized suspicion at all. In the latter two cases, the Court suggested that searches designed to prevent harm to the public safety should be easier to justify than searches seeking evidence for criminal cases.

Exaggerated fear of Big Brother

Proposals to increase the government's wiretapping powers awaken fears of unleashing Orwellian thought police[3] to spy on, harass, blackmail, and smear political dissenters and others. Libertarians point out that most conversations overheard and e-mails intercepted in the war on terrorism will be innocent and that the tappers and buggers will overhear intimacies and embarrassing disclosures that are none of the government's business.

Such concerns argue for taking care to broaden wiretapping and surveillance powers only as much as seems reasonable to prevent terrorist acts. But broader wiretapping authority is not all bad for civil liberties. It is a more accurate and benign method of penetrating terrorist cells than the main alternative, which is planting and recruiting informers—a dangerous, ugly, and unreliable business in which the government is already free to engage without limit. The narrower the government's surveillance powers, the more it will rely on informants.

Moreover, curbing the government's power to collect information through wiretapping is not the only way to protect against misuse of the information. Numerous other safeguards less damaging to the counterterrorism effort—inspectors general, the Justice Department's Office of Professional Responsibility, congressional investigators, a gaggle of liberal and conservative civil liberties groups, and the news media—have become extremely potent. The FBI has very little incentive to waste time and resources on unwarranted snooping.

To keep the specter of Big Brother in perspective, it's worth recalling that the president had unlimited power to wiretap suspected foreign spies and terrorists until 1978 (when FISA was adopted); if this devastated privacy or liberty, hardly anyone noticed. It's also worth noting that despite the government's already-vast power to comb through computerized records of our banking and commercial transactions and much else that we do in the computer age, the vast majority of the people who have seen their privacy or reputations shredded have not been wronged by rogue officials. They have been wronged by media organizations, which do far greater damage to far more people with far less accountability.

Nineteen years ago, in *The Rise of the Computer State*, David Burnham wrote: "The question looms before us: Can the United States continue to flourish and grow in an age when the physical movements, individual purchases, conversations and meetings of every citizen are constantly under surveillance by private companies and government agencies?" It can. It has. And now that the computer state has risen indeed, the threat of being watched by Big Brother or smeared by the FBI seems a lot smaller than the threat of being blown to bits or poisoned by terrorists.

The case for coercive interrogation

The same Zacarias Moussaoui whose possessions would have been searched but for FISA's undue stringency also epitomizes another problem: the perverse impact of the rules—or what are widely assumed to be

---

3. In George Orwell's novel, *1984*, a totalitarian government—referred to as Big Brother—exercises complete control over citizens lives, including their thoughts.

the rules—restricting interrogations of suspected terrorists.

"We were prevented from even attempting to question Moussaoui on the day of the attacks when, in theory, he could have possessed further information about other co-conspirators," Coleen Rowley complained in a little-noticed portion of her May 21, [2002] letter to Mueller. The reason was that Moussaoui had requested a lawyer. To the FBI that meant that any further interrogation would violate the Fifth Amendment *"Miranda rules"* laid down by the Supreme Court in 1966 and subsequent cases.

It's not hard to imagine such rules (or such an interpretation) leading to the loss of countless lives. While interrogating Moussaoui on September 11 might not have yielded any useful information, suppose that he had been part of a team planning a second wave of hijackings later in September and that his resistance could have been cracked. Or suppose that the FBI learns tomorrow, from a wiretap, that another al-Qaida team is planning an imminent attack and arrests an occupant of the wiretapped apartment.

The danger that a preventive-detention regime for suspected terrorists would take us too far down the slippery slope . . . is simply not as bad as letting would-be mass murderers roam the country.

We all know the drill. Before asking any questions, FBI agents (and police) must warn the suspect: "You have a right to remain silent." And if the suspect asks for a lawyer, all interrogation must cease until the lawyer arrives (and tells the suspect to keep quiet). This seems impossible to justify when dealing with people suspected of planning mass murder. But it's the law, isn't it?

Actually, it's not the law, though many judges think it is, along with most lawyers, federal agents, police, and cop-show mavens. You do *not* have a right to remain silent. The most persuasive interpretation of the Constitution and the Supreme Courts' precedents is that agents and police are free to interrogate any suspect without *Miranda* warnings; to spurn requests for a lawyer; to press bald for answers; and—at least in a terrorism investigation—perhaps even to use hours of interrogation, verbal abuse, isolation, blindfolds, polygraph tests, death-penalty threats, and other forms of psychological coercion short of torture or physical brutality. Maybe even truth serum.

The Fifth Amendment self-incrimination clause says only that no person "shall be compelled in any criminal case to be a witness against himself." The clause prohibits forcing a defendant to testify at his trial and also making him a witness against himself indirectly by using compelled pretrial statements. It does not prohibit compelling a suspect to talk. *Miranda* held only that in determining whether a defendant's statements (and information derived from them) may be used against him at his trial, courts must treat all interrogations of arrested suspects as inherently coercive unless the warnings are given.

Courts typically ignore this distinction because in almost every litigated case the issue is whether a criminal defendant's incriminating statements should be suppressed at his trial; there is no need to focus on whether the constitutional problem is the conduct of the interrogation, or the use at trial of evidence obtained, or both. And as a matter of verbal shorthand, it's a lot easier to say "the police violated *Miranda*" than to say "the judge would be violating *Miranda* if he or she were to admit the defendant's statements into evidence at his trial."

But the war against terrorism has suddenly increased the significance of this previously academic question. In terrorism investigations, it will often be more important to get potentially lifesaving information from a suspect than to get incriminating statements for use in court.

Fortunately for terrorism investigators, the Supreme Court said in 1990 that "a constitutional violation [of the Fifth Amendment's self-incrimination clause] occurs only at trial." It cited an earlier ruling that the government can obtain court orders compelling reluctant witnesses to talk and can imprison them for contempt of court if they refuse, if it first guarantees them immunity from prosecution on the basis of their statements or any derivative evidence. These decisions support the conclusion that the self-incrimination clause "does not forbid the forcible extraction of information but only the use of information so extracted as evidence in a criminal case," as a federal appeals court ruled in 1992.

Of course, even when the primary reason for questioning a suspected terrorist is prevention, the government could pay a heavy cost for ignoring *Miranda* and using coercive interrogation techniques, because it would sometimes find it difficult or impossible to prosecute extremely dangerous terrorists. But terrorism investigators may be able to get their evidence and use it too, if the Court—or Congress, which unlike the Court would not have to wait for a proper case to come along—extends a 1984 precedent creating what the justices called a "public safety" exception to *Miranda*. That decision allowed use at trial of a defendant's incriminating answer to a policeman's demand (before any *Miranda* warnings) to know where his gun was hidden.

Those facts are not a perfect parallel for most terrorism investigations, because of the immediate nature of the danger (an accomplice might pick up the gun) and the spontaneity of the officer's question. And as Rowley testified, "In order to give timely advice" about what an agent can legally do, "you've got to run to a computer and pull it up, and I think that many people have kind of forgotten that case, and many courts have actually limited it to its facts."

The question is not whether we should increase governmental power. . . . The question is how much.

But when the main purpose of the interrogation is to prevent terrorist attacks, the magnitude of the danger argues for a broader public safety exception, as Rowley implied in her letter.

Congress should neither wait for the justices to clarify the law nor assume that they will reach the right conclusions without prodding. It should make the rules as clear as possible as soon as possible. Officials like Rowley need to know that they are free to interrogate suspected terrorists more aggressively than they suppose. While a law expanding the public safety exception to *Miranda* would be challenged as unconstitutional, it would contradict no existing Supreme Court precedent and—if carefully calibrated to apply only when the immediate purpose is to save lives— would probably be upheld.

Would investigators routinely ignore *Miranda* and engage in coercive interrogation—perhaps extorting false confessions—if told that the legal restraints were far looser than had been supposed? The risk would not be significantly greater than it is now. Police would still need to comply with *Miranda* in almost all cases for fear of jeopardizing any prosecution. While that would not be true in terrorism investigations if the public safety exception were broadened, extreme abuses such as beatings and torture would violate the due process clause of the Fifth Amendment (and of the Fourteenth Amendment as well), which has been construed as barring interrogation techniques that "shock the conscience," and is backed up by administrative penalties and the threat of civil lawsuits.

Bringing preventive detention inside the law

Of all the erosions of civil liberties that must be considered since September 11, preventive detention—incarcerating people because of their perceived dangerousness even when they are neither convicted nor charged with any crime—would represent the sharpest departure from centuries of Anglo-American jurisprudence and come closest to police statism.

But the case for some kind of preventive detention has never been as strong. Al-Qaida's capacity to inflict catastrophic carnage dwarfs any previous domestic security threat. Its "sleeper" agents are trained to avoid criminal activities that might arouse suspicion. So the careful ones cannot be arrested on criminal charges until it is too late. And their lust for martyrdom renders criminal punishment ineffective as a deterrent.

Without preventive detention, the Bush administration would apparently have no solid legal basis for holding the two U.S. citizens in military brigs in this country as suspected "enemy combatants"—or for holding the more than 500 noncitizens at Guantanamo Bay [Cuba]. Nor would it have had a solid legal basis for detaining any of the 19 September 11 hijackers if it had suspected them of links to al-Qaida before they struck. Nor could it legally have detained Moussaoui—who was suspected of terrorist intent but was implicated in no provable crime or conspiracy—had he had not overstayed his visa.

What should the government do when it is convinced of a suspect's terrorist intent but lacks admissible evidence of any crime? Or when a criminal trial would blow vital intelligence secrets? Or when ambiguous evidence makes it a tossup whether a suspect is harmless or an al-Qaidan? What should it do with suspects like Jose Padilla, who was arrested in Chicago and is now in military detention because he is suspected of (but not charged with) plotting a radioactive "dirty-bomb" attack on Washington, D.C.? Or with a (hypothetical) Pakistani graduate student in chemistry, otherwise unremarkable, who has downloaded articles about how terrorists might use small planes to start an anthrax epidemic and shown an intense but unexplained interest in crop-dusters?

Only four options exist. Let such suspects go about their business unmonitored until (perhaps) they commit mass murders; assign agents to tail them until (perhaps) they give the agents the slip; bring prosecutions without solid evidence and risk acquittals; and preventive detention. The last could theoretically include not only incarceration but milder restraints such as house arrest or restriction to certain areas combined with agreement to carry (or to be implanted with) a device enabling the government to track the suspect's movements at all times.

As an alternative to preventive detention, Congress could seek to facilitate prosecutions of suspected "sleepers" by allowing use of now-inadmissible and secret evidence and stretching the already broad concept of criminal conspiracy so far as to make it almost a thought crime. But that would have a harsher effect on innocent terrorism suspects than would preventive detention and could weaken protections for all criminal defendants.

As Alan Dershowitz notes, "[N]o civilized nation confronting serious danger has ever relied exclusively on criminal convictions for past offenses. Every country has introduced, by one means or another, a system of preventive or administrative detention for persons who are thought to be dangerous but who might not be convictable under the conventional criminal law."

The best argument against preventive detention of suspected international terrorists is history's warning that the system will be abused, could expand inexorably—especially in the panic that might follow future attacks—and has such terrifying potential for infecting the entire criminal justice system and undermining our Bill of Rights that we should never start down that road. What is terrorist intent, and how may it be proved? Through a suspect's advocacy of a terrorist group's cause? Association with its members or sympathizers? If preventive detention is okay for people suspected of (but not charged with) terrorist intent, what about people suspected of homicidal intent, or violent proclivities, or dealing drugs?

These are serious concerns. But the dangers of punishing dissident speech, guilt by association, and overuse of preventive detention could be controlled by careful legislation. This would not be the first exception to the general rule against preventive detention. The others have worked fairly well. They include pretrial detention without bail of criminal defendants found to be dangerous, civil commitment of people found dangerous by reason of mental illness, and medical quarantines, a practice that may once again be necessary in the event of bioterrorism. All in all, the danger that a preventive-detention regime for suspected terrorists would take us too far down the slippery slope toward police statism is simply not as bad as the danger of letting would-be mass murderers roam the country.

In any event, we already have a preventive-detention regime for suspected international terrorists—three regimes, in fact, all created and controlled by the Bush administration without congressional input. First, two U.S. citizens—Jose Padilla, the suspected would-be dirty bomber arrested in Chicago, and Yaser Esam Hamdi, a Louisiana-born Saudi Arabian captured in Afghanistan and taken first to Guantanamo—have been in military brigs in this country for many months without being charged with any crime or allowed to see any lawyer or any judge. The administration claims that it never has to prove anything to anyone. It says that even U.S. citizens arrested in this country—who may have far stronger grounds than battlefield detainees for denying that they are enemy combatants—are entitled to no due process whatever once the government puts that label on them. This argument is virtually unprecedented, wrong as a matter of law, and indefensible as a matter of policy.

Second, Attorney General John Ashcroft rounded up more than 1,100 mostly Muslim noncitizens in the fall of 2001, which involved preventive detention in many cases although they were charged with immigration violations or crimes (mostly minor) or held under the material witness statute. This when-in-doubt-detain approach effectively reversed the presumption of innocence in the hope of disrupting any planned follow-up attacks. We may never know whether it succeeded in this vital objective. But the legal and moral bases for holding hundreds of apparently harmless detainees, sometimes without access to legal counsel, in conditions of unprecedented secrecy, seemed less and less plausible as weeks and months went by. Worse, the administration treated many (if not most) of the detainees shabbily and some abusively. (By mid-2002, the vast majority had been deported or released.)

Third, the Pentagon has incarcerated hundreds of Arab and other prisoners captured in Afghanistan at Guantanamo, apparently to avoid the jurisdiction of all courts—and has refused to create a fair, credible process for determining which are in fact enemy combatants and which of those are "unlawful."

These three regimes have been implemented with little regard for the law, for the rights of the many (mostly former) detainees who are probably innocent, or for international opinion. It is time for Congress to step in—to authorize a regime of temporary preventive detention for suspected international terrorists, while circumscribing that regime and specifying strong safeguards against abuse.

Civil liberties for a new era

It is senseless to adhere to overly broad restrictions imposed by decades-old civil-liberties rules when confronting the threat of unprecedented carnage at the hands of modern terrorists. In the words of Harvard Law School's Laurence H. Tribe, "The old adage that it is better to free 100 guilty men than to imprison one innocent describes a calculus that our Constitution—which is no suicide pact—does not impose on government when the 100 who are freed belong to terrorist cells that slaughter innocent civilians, and may well have access to chemical, biological, or nuclear weapons." The question is not whether we should increase governmental power to meet such dangers. The question is how much.

3

The PATRIOT Act Has Helped Prevent Terrorist Attacks

Alice Fisher

Alice Fisher is a deputy attorney general for the U.S. Department of Justice.

The USA PATRIOT Act, enacted on October 26, 2001, in response to the September 11, 2001, terrorist attacks on America, has been an invaluable aid to law enforcement. The act has removed important obstacles to investigating terrorism. For example, section 219 of the act allows federal judges to issue nationwide search warrants in terrorism investigations, whereas prior to the act investigators had to expend crucial time and effort procuring multiple warrants from different judges in different jurisdictions. The act has also greatly strengthened criminal laws against terrorism, particularly laws aimed at the individuals who finance and support terrorist groups. Finally, the act has removed many restrictions on law enforcement's ability to gather intelligence through physical searches, wiretaps, electronic surveillance, and increased access to criminal records.

Distinguished members of the Senate Judiciary Subcommittee on Technology, Terrorism and Government Information, I am honored to appear before you to testify about the Department of Justice's implementation and use of the important anti-terrorism provisions in the USA PATRIOT Act. I want to thank this Subcommittee's members, who helped to develop and enact the USA PATRIOT so swiftly in the wake of [the September 11, 2001, terrorist attacks]. As Deputy Assistant Attorney General of the Criminal Division, with responsibility over the Terrorism and Violent Crimes Section, I have been personally involved in seeing that the tools Congress provided in the Act have been used as intended: to enhance the ability of law enforcement to bring terrorists and other criminals to justice.

The unprecedented and heinous attacks on our nation, in which over three thousand innocent civilians were killed in New York City, in Pennsylvania, and at the Pentagon, occurred just over one year ago. At that time,

Alice Fisher, testimony before the Senate Committee on the Judiciary, October 9, 2002.

the President pledged to the American people that we would not relent until justice was done and our nation was secure. Members of this Committee, and the Congress in general, joined the President [George W. Bush] as key partners in this important undertaking. Congress's swift and comprehensive response, through passage of the USA PATRIOT Act, provided us with vital new tools, and updated those tools already at our disposal, that have been instrumental to our efforts to combat terrorism in the most extensive criminal investigation in history. As the President stated when he signed the USA PATRIOT Act on October 26, 2001, we took "an essential step in defeating terrorism, while protecting the constitutional rights of Americans." One year later, I am pleased to report that we have used these tools effectively, aggressively and responsibly.

Implementing the USA PATRIOT Act

As the Attorney General [John Ashcroft] told the Senate Judiciary Committee in July, the Department's single and overarching goal since September 11 has been to prevent future terrorist attacks on the United States and its citizens. We have been aggressively implementing the USA PATRIOT Act from the outset. Following its passage, we immediately sent field guidance to United States Attorney's offices, advising them of the Act's new authorities and urging their use, where appropriate, in investigating and prosecuting terrorism and other criminal acts. We have followed up with additional guidance and training over the past year, and we consult informally with federal prosecutors and investigators at work in the field investigating suspected terrorists. Our manual proved invaluable in ensuring that prosecutors around the country could immediately benefit from and utilize the new law enforcement tools provided by the Act.

Congress's swift . . . passage of the USA PATRIOT Act, provided us with vital new tools . . . that have been instrumental in our efforts to combat terrorism in the most extensive criminal investigation in history.

Law enforcement has been engaged in an ongoing cooperative effort to identify, disrupt and dismantle terrorist networks. We are expending every effort and devoting all available resources to intercept terrorists and defend our nation. Never was this so apparent as last Friday [October 4, 2002], a defining day in the war on terrorism, when we neutralized a suspected terrorist cell in Portland, Oregon, convicted attempted suicide bomber Richard Reid, and saw John Walker Lindh, an American captured fighting for the Taliban in Afghanistan, sentenced to twenty years' imprisonment. In the last six weeks, we have charged 17 individuals involved in terrorism-related activities. In addition to Portland, we have broken up terrorist cells in Detroit and Buffalo, and we have charged an individual with attempting to set up an Al Qaeda terrorist training camp in Oregon. Enhanced penalties authorized by the USA PATRIOT Act have proven an important tool in all of these cases.

Today, I will provide a brief summary of the Department's work to date implementing the new powers authorized by the USA PATRIOT Act. I cannot, of course, disclose information that might compromise or undermine ongoing criminal investigations and prosecutions. However, I can discuss a number of areas in which the Department of Justice, in conjunction with other departments and agencies, is making meaningful headway in the war on terrorism. In particular, over the past year [since September 11, 2001], the Department has used the following important new authorities and tools provided by the Act:

- we have charged a number of individuals with crimes under 18 U.S.C. §§2339A and 2339B, which prohibit providing material support to terrorists or terrorist organizations, and carry enhanced penalties;
- we have used newly streamlined authority to use trap and trace orders to track communications of a number of criminals, including the terrorist kidnappers and murderers of journalist Daniel Pearl, as well as identity thieves and a four-time murderer;
- we have used new authority to subpoena information about Internet users' network addresses to track down terrorists and computer hackers;
- we have used newly authorized nationwide search warrants for terrorist investigations at least three times, including during the ongoing anthrax investigation;
- we have utilized provisions in the Act to foster an unprecedented level of cooperation and information sharing between government agencies; and
- we have saved precious time and resources through a provision that permits officials to obtain court orders for electronic surveillance pertaining to a particular suspect, rather than a particular device.

I will focus my testimony on four key areas in which the USA PATRIOT Act has aided law enforcement efforts: (1) it updated the law to reflect new technology; (2) it removed obstacles to investigating terrorism; (3) it strengthened criminal laws and enhanced penalties; and (4) it facilitated increased intelligence sharing, gathering and analyzing. The fifth key area, protecting our borders, falls within the bailiwick of the INS [Immigration and Naturalization Service]. . . .

Internet surveillance

1. Updating the Law to Reflect New Technology. First, the USA PATRIOT Act allowed us to modernize our badly outmoded surveillance tools. Terrorists engaged in covert multinational operations use advanced technology, particularly in their communications and planning. While terrorists who were plotting against our nation traveled across the globe, carrying laptop computers and using disposable cell phones, federal investigators operated under laws seemingly frozen in an era of telegrams and switchboard operators. Prior to September 11, we operated both at a technological disadvantage and under legal barriers that severely restricted our surveillance capabilities. In particular, we did not have sufficiently sophisticated abilities to monitor communications in either the digital or analog world, and law enforcement officials operated under onerous rules that hindered their ability to conduct investigations in a timely manner. The USA PA-

TRIOT Act modernized existing law, and gave investigators crucial new tools to deal with these problems. We have put this new authority to good use.

Prior to the USA PATRIOT Act, for example, federal law required officers to spend critical time going through the burdensome process of obtaining wiretap orders to access unopened voice-mail. Now, just as had already been the case with email messages, pursuant to section 209 of the PATRIOT Act, officers can use search warrants to expedite the seizure of voice mail. Federal investigators have used these warrants in a variety of criminal cases, including both foreign and domestic terrorism cases.

Before the PATRIOT Act . . . officers' access to critical information in the Internet era was unnecessarily delayed and obstructed.

Similarly, section 220 of the Act, which permits a law enforcement officer to execute a search warrant for electronic evidence outside of the district that issued the warrant, has proved crucial to dealing with the post-September 11 deluge of search warrant applications seeking evidence stored in computers, or transmitted through the Internet. Before the PATRIOT Act, because a court sitting in one district could not issue a warrant that was valid in another district, officers' access to critical information in the Internet era was unnecessarily delayed and obstructed, as the physical infrastructure, such as servers used by Internet service providers, were often located thousands of miles from the scene of the crime under investigation. Even though the Internet is a far-flung communications network, with access available to anyone with a properly equipped personal computer, the federal courts in those districts in which ISPs [Internet Service Providers] happened to locate their servers (such as in northern California) were required to handle requests for warrants in investigations all across the country. The efficiency resulting from the Act's simple modifications to existing law was invaluable in several time-sensitive investigations, including one involving a dangerous fugitive and another involving a hacker who used stolen trade secrets to extort a company.

The USA PATRIOT Act also modernized the legal requirements for pen register and trap and trace orders, streamlining this authority by clarifying that it can be used in a variety of new communications forms, not just on telephone lines, and by permitting a single order nationwide. These devices—which reveal, for example, the numbers dialed by a particular telephone or the email address to which an account sends messages—allow investigators to identify patterns of suspicious behavior or connections with known terrorists or terrorist organizations. The Department has used this improved tool to trace communications of a number of criminals, including kidnappers who communicated their demands via email, terrorist conspirators, at least one major drug distributor, identity thieves, a four-time murderer, and a fugitive who fled on the eve of trial using a fake passport. This new provision also allowed prosecutors in the Daniel Pearl case to get information critical in the identification of some of those individuals responsible for his kidnaping and murder.

The USA PATRIOT Act has updated federal law for the digital era by expediting the government's ability to execute orders requiring the help of third parties, such as telecommunications companies, in terrorism investigations. Under previous law, if an officer wanted to enlist the help of third parties to monitor a suspect, the officer had to seek specific court orders for every information source the suspect could potentially utilize. Section 206 of the Act abolished this requirement by permitting officers to simply obtain a court order pertaining to the suspect, not the particular device or devices used. This new authority allows us to avoid unnecessary cat-and-mouse games with terrorists who are trained to thwart surveillance by rapidly changing hotels or residences, cell phones, and Internet accounts before important meetings or communications.

Other provisions, such as section 211, which clarifies that the Electronic Communications Privacy Act, not the Cable Act, governs the disclosure of information regarding communication services provided by cable companies, and section 212, which allows Internet providers to disclose records to law enforcement in emergencies presenting a risk to life or limb, have made it much easier for third party communication providers to assist law enforcement without fear of civil liability. The latter authority, for example, allowed us to track down a student who posted electronic bulletin board threats to bomb his high school and shoot a faculty member and several students. Afraid of being sued, the owner and operator of the Internet message board initially resisted disclosing to federal law enforcement officials the evidence that could lead to the identification of the threat-maker. However, after he was told about the new USA PATRIOT Act emergency authority, he voluntarily disclosed to law enforcement Internet addressing information that was instrumental in the student's timely arrest and confession and in preventing the student from potentially carrying out his violent threats.

Finally, the USA PATRIOT Act has brought the federal wiretap statute into the 21st century by adding terrorism crimes to the list of offenses for which wiretap orders are available. These provisions have proven extremely useful to law enforcement officials. At least one recent wiretap order has been issued based on this expanded list of terrorism offenses. We believe that these enhancements will bring more terrorists to justice and prevent them from inflicting major damage on the infrastructure of telecommunications providers.

Facilitating timely investigations

2. Removing Obstacles to Investigating Terrorism. Second, the USA PATRIOT Act has removed various obstacles to investigating terrorism and has greatly enhanced the Department's ability to thwart, disrupt, weaken, and eliminate the infrastructure of terrorist organizations. Section 219, for example, which allows federal judges to issue nationwide search warrants for physical searches in terrorism investigations, has enabled investigators to avoid expending precious time petitioning multiple judges in multiple districts for warrants. We have used this provision at least three times, including during the ongoing anthrax investigation. In that case, agents were able to obtain a search warrant from a federal judge in Washington, D.C. in order to investigate the premises of America Media, Inc.

in Boca Raton, Florida. Timely action is often of the essence in law enforcement investigations and this new authority will prove invaluable.

Prior to the USA PATRIOT Act, we faced significant barriers in our ability to exclude or remove terrorists because of various statutory loopholes in the definitions concerning terrorism. Section 411 of the USA PATRIOT Act addressed these problems by expanding the grounds of inadmissibility of aliens to include those who provide assistance to terrorist organizations. At the Attorney General's request, the Department of State has listed 46 entities as terrorist organizations pursuant to authority under this provision. Members of these organizations are now denied admission to the United States for any purpose.

Title III of the USA PATRIOT Act provides law enforcement with important new authority to . . . seize terrorist assets, both foreign and domestic.

We believe that a number of other areas, such as greater authority to collect DNA samples from federal prisoners convicted of certain terrorism offenses under section 503, greater ability to pay rewards to help punish terrorists under sections 501 and 502, enhanced capabilities to investigate computer fraud pursuant to section 506, which permits joint Secret Service-FBI cooperation in investigations, and greater access to education information and statistics under sections 507 and 508, likewise will prove very useful in our efforts. While we have not yet had to use all of the Act's provisions, we know that they will serve as vital tools should the need arise.

3. Strengthening the Criminal Laws against Terrorism. Third, the USA PATRIOT Act substantially strengthened criminal law, helping us pursue criminals in the most extensive criminal investigation in history. Critical to our efforts is the enhanced ability to prosecute and punish terrorists captured abroad as well as those arrested within our borders. These provisions have proven to be powerful new weapons in our fight against international terrorism as well as other kinds of international criminal activity.

Targeting terrorist financing

Enhanced criminal laws relating to terrorist financing, for example, have provided an effective tool in getting law enforcement inserted into the early stages of terrorist planning. Title III of the USA PATRIOT Act provides law enforcement with important new authority to investigate and prosecute the financing of terrorism. We can now seize terrorist assets, both foreign and domestic, if the property or its owner is involved in, related to, or in support of acts of domestic or international terrorism. It is now a crime for anyone subject to U.S. jurisdiction to provide anything of value—including their own efforts or expertise—to organizations designated as "foreign terrorist organization." This is true regardless of whether the persons providing such support intend their donations to be used for violent purposes, or whether actual terrorism results. If someone subject to U.S. jurisdiction provides, or even attempts to provide, any material support or resources to Hamas, Hizballah, Al Qaeda, the Abu Sayyaf

Group or any of the other designated groups, that person can be prosecuted. And our prosecutors do not have to prove that the support actually went to specific terrorist acts. The Department has used this provision in prosecuting a number of Al Qaeda associated individuals and in breaking up terrorist cells in this country. For example, John Walker Lindh, the American citizen who joined the Taliban [the Afghan regime harboring al-Qaeda terrorists] and was captured by military forces in Afghanistan, was charged with 10 counts, including a total of six relating to providing material support to individuals and to organizations that commit crimes of terrorism. Lindh, who pled guilty to providing services to the Taliban and to carrying an explosive while engaged in the commission of a felony, was sentenced last Friday [October 4, 2002] to 20 years imprisonment. On August 28, 2002, we charged Ernest James Ujaama with providing material support to Al Qaeda by, among other things, attempting to set up an Al Qaeda terrorist training camp at a farm in Oregon. On that same day, five Detroit men affiliated with Al Qaeda were charged with providing material support or resources to terrorists. On September 13, 2002, six United States citizens in the Buffalo area, who are believed to be part of another Al Qaeda-affiliated cell, were arrested on charges of providing support or resources to terrorists. And just last Friday [October 4, 2002] we indicted six individuals in Portland, Oregon, also affiliated with Al Qaeda, with providing material support or resources to terrorists.

Our ability to fight transnational crime was further enhanced by making the smuggling of bulk cash across our border unlawful, adding terrorism and other offenses to the list of racketeering offenses, and providing prosecutors with the authority to seize money subject to forfeiture in a foreign bank account by authorizing the seizure of such a foreign bank's funds held in a U.S. correspondent account. Another important provision expanded our ability to prosecute unlicenced money transmitters by enhancing section 1960 of Title 18. We used this revised statute successfully in the District of Massachusetts. On November 18, 2001, a federal grand jury returned an indictment charging Liban Hussein, the local president of an Al Barakaat money remitting house, and his brother, Mohamed Hussein, with a violation of § 1960. This prosecution was part of a national, and indeed international, enforcement action against the Al Barakaat network, which has financed the operations of Al Qaeda and other terrorist organizations. Mohamed Hussein was convicted and sentenced to 18 months' incarceration for operating an unlicenced money remitting business. His brother is a fugitive.

Title III of the Act also permits the forfeiture of funds held in United States interbank accounts. We used this provision to prosecute James Gibson, who had defrauded clients of millions of dollars by fraudulently structuring settlement for numerous personal injury victims. After he and his wife fled to Belize and deposited some of the monies from the scheme in two Belizean banks, we were able to have a seizure warrant served on the bank's interbank account in the United States and recover remaining funds.

We have attempted to use section 801, which makes it a federal offense to engage in terrorist attacks and other acts of violence against mass transportation systems, in at least one high profile case. One of the counts brought against "shoe bomber" Richard Reid, who was charged for concealing a bomb in his shoe during a transatlantic flight, alleged a violation

4

The PATRIOT Act Has Undermined Civil Liberties

Nancy Chang

Nancy Chang is senior litigation attorney for the Center for Constitutional Rights, a civil liberties advocacy organization based in New York City.

The USA PATRIOT Act, passed hastily in October 2001, contains several radical measures that sacrifice political freedoms in the name of homeland security. The act creates a new, poorly defined federal crime called "domestic terrorism" that could be interpreted to include almost any opposition to government policies. The act also gives government agencies broad new license to evade the Fourth Amendment and invade Americans' privacy through electronic surveillance and covert searches of homes and offices. The reasoning behind the USA PATRIOT Act, which uses the narrowest possible interpretation of the Bill of Rights to justify homeland security measures, is extremist and likely to lead to further erosion of political freedom.

Just six weeks after the September 11 [2001] terrorist attacks on the World Trade Center and the Pentagon, a jittery Congress—exiled from its anthrax-contaminated offices and confronted with warnings that more terrorist assaults were soon to come—capitulated to the Bush Administration's demands for a new arsenal of anti-terrorism weapons. Over vigorous objections from civil liberties organizations on both ends of the political spectrum, Congress overwhelmingly approved the Uniting and Strengthening America by Providing Appropriate Tools Required to Intercept and Obstruct Terrorism Act, better known by its acronym, the USA PATRIOT Act. The House vote was 356-to-66, and the Senate vote was 98-to-1. Along the way, the Republican House leadership, in a raw display of force, jettisoned an anti-terrorism bill that the House Judiciary Committee had unanimously approved and that would have addressed a number of civil liberties concerns. The hastily-drafted, complex, and far-reaching legislation spans 342 pages. Yet it was passed with virtually no public

Nancy Chang, "The USA PATRIOT Act: What's So Patriotic About Trampling on the Bill of Rights?" www.ccr-ny.org, November 2001. Copyright © 2001 by Nancy Chang. Reproduced by permission.

hearing or debate, and it was accompanied by neither a conference nor a committee report. On October 26, the Act was signed into law by a triumphant President George W. Bush.

Radical measures

Although a number of its provisions are not controversial, the USA PATRIOT Act nevertheless stands out as radical in its design. To an unprecedented degree, the Act sacrifices our political freedoms in the name of national security and upsets the democratic values that define our nation by consolidating vast new powers in the executive branch of government. The Act enhances the executive's ability to conduct surveillance and gather intelligence, places an array of new tools at the disposal of the prosecution, including new crimes, enhanced penalties, and longer statutes of limitations, and grants the Immigration and Naturalization Service (INS) the authority to detain immigrants suspected of terrorism for lengthy, and in some cases indefinite, periods of time. And at the same time that the Act inflates the powers of the executive, it insulates the exercise of these powers from meaningful judicial and Congressional oversight.

The [PATRIOT] Act sacrifices our political freedoms in the name of national security and upsets the democratic values that define our nation.

It remains to be seen how the executive will wield its new authority. However, if the two months that have elapsed since September 11 serve as a guide, we should brace ourselves for a flagrant disregard of the rule of law by those charged with its enforcement. Already, the Department of Justice (DOJ) has admitted to detaining more than 1,100 immigrants, not one of whom has been charged with committing a terrorist act and only a handful of whom are being held as material witnesses to the September 11 hijackings. Many in this group appear to have been held for extended time periods under an extraordinary interim regulation announced by Attorney General John Ashcroft on September 17 and published in Federal Register on September 20. This regulation sets aside the strictures of due process by permitting the INS to detain aliens without charge for 48 hours or an uncapped "additional reasonable period of time" in the event of an "emergency or other extraordinary circumstance." Also, many in this group are being held without bond under the pretext of unrelated criminal charges or minor immigration violations, in a modern-day form of preventive detention. Chillingly, the Attorney General's response to the passage of the USA PATRIOT Act was not a pledge to use his new powers responsibly and guard against their abuse, but instead was a vow to step up his detention efforts. Conflating immigrant status with terrorist status, he declared: "Let the terrorists among us be warned, if you overstay your visas even by one day, we will arrest you."

Furthermore, the Administration has made no secret of its hope that the judiciary will accede to its broad reading of the USA PATRIOT Act just as pliantly as Congress acceded to its broad legislative agenda. In a letter sent to key Senators while Congress was considering this legislation, Assistant Attorney General Daniel J. Bryant, of DOJ's Office of Legislative Affairs, openly advocated for a suspension of the Fourth Amendment's warrant requirement in the government's investigation of foreign national security threats. The Bryant letter brazenly declares:

> As Commander-in-Chief, *the President must be able to use whatever means necessary to prevent attacks upon the United States;* this power, by implication, includes the authority to collect information necessary to its effective exercise. . . . The government's interest has changed from merely conducting foreign intelligence surveillance to counter intelligence operations by other nations, to one of preventing terrorist attacks against American citizens and property within the continental United States itself. The courts have observed that even the use of deadly force is reasonable under the Fourth Amendment if used in self-defense or to protect others. . . . Here, for Fourth Amendment purposes, the right to self-defense is not that of an individual, but that of the nation and its citizens. . . . *If the government's heightened interest in self-defense justifies the use of deadly force, then it certainly would also justify warrantless searches.* [Emphasis added.]

The Administration's blatant power grab, coupled with the wide array of anti-terrorism tools that the USA PATRIOT Act puts at its disposal, portends a wholesale suspension of civil liberties that will reach far beyond those who are involved in terrorist activities. First, the Act places our First Amendment rights to freedom of speech and political association in jeopardy by creating a broad new crime of "domestic terrorism," and by denying entry to non-citizens on the basis of ideology. Second, the Act will reduce our already lowered expectations of privacy under the Fourth Amendment by granting the government enhanced surveillance powers. Third, non-citizens will see a further erosion of their due process rights as they are placed in mandatory detention and removed from the United States under the Act. Political activists who are critical of our government or who maintain ties with international political movements, in addition to immigrants, are likely to bear the brunt of these attacks on our civil liberties.

Silencing political dissent

Section 802 of the USA PATRIOT Act defines for the first time a federal crime of "domestic terrorism" that broadly extends to "acts dangerous to human life that are a violation of the criminal laws" if they "appear to be intended . . . to influence the policy of a government by intimidation or coercion," and if they "occur primarily within the territorial jurisdiction of the United States." Because this definition is couched in such vague and expansive terms, it may well be read by federal law enforcement agencies as licensing the investigation and surveillance of political activists and organizations based on their opposition to government policies. It also may be read by prosecutors as licensing the criminalization of legitimate political dissent. Vigorous protest activities, by their very nature, could be construed as acts that "appear to be intended . . . to influence the policy of a government by intimidation or coercion." Further, clashes between demonstrators and police officers and acts of civil disobedience—even those that do not result in injuries and are entirely non-violent—could be construed as "dangerous to human life" and in "violation of the criminal laws." Environmental activists, anti-globalization activists, and anti-abortion activists who use direct action to further their political agendas are particularly vulnerable to prosecution as "domestic terrorists."

Environmental activists, anti-globalization activists, and anti-abortion activists who use direct action to further their political agendas are particularly vulnerable to prosecution as "domestic terrorists."

In addition, political activists and the organizations with which they associate may unwittingly find themselves the subject of unwanted government attention in the form of surveillance and other intelligence-gathering operations. The manner in which the government implements the Act must be carefully monitored to ascertain whether activists and organizations are being targeted selectively for surveillance and prosecution based on their opposition to government policies. The First Amendment does not tolerate viewpoint-based discrimination.

Furthermore, Section 411 of the Act poses an ideological test for entry into the United States that takes into consideration core political speech. Representatives of a political or social group "whose public endorsement of acts of terrorist activity the Secretary of State has determined undermines United States efforts to reduce or eliminate terrorist activities" can no longer gain entry into the United States. Entry is also barred to non-citizens who have used their "position of prominence within any country to endorse or espouse terrorist activity," if the Secretary of State determines that their speech "undermines United States efforts to reduce or eliminate terrorist activities."

Enhanced surveillance powers

The USA PATRIOT Act launches a three-pronged assault on our privacy. First, the Act grants the executive branch unprecedented, and largely unchecked, surveillance powers, including the enhanced ability to track email and Internet usage, conduct sneak-and-peek searches, obtain sensitive personal records, monitor financial transactions, and conduct nationwide roving wiretaps. Second, the Act permits law enforcement agencies to circumvent the Fourth Amendment's requirement of probable cause when conducting wiretaps and searches that have, as "a significant purpose," the gathering of foreign intelligence. Third, the Act allows for the sharing of information between criminal and intelligence operations and thereby opens the door to a resurgence of domestic spying by the Central Intelligence Agency.

By and large, Congress granted the Administration its longstanding wish list of enhanced surveillance tools, coupled with the ability to use these tools with only minimal judicial and Congressional oversight. In its rush to pass an anti-terrorism bill, Congress failed to exact in exchange a showing that these highly intrusive new tools are actually needed to combat terrorism and that the Administration can be trusted not to abuse them.

The [June 2001] decision in *Kyllo v. United States* serves as a pointed reminder that once a Fourth Amendment protection has been eroded, the resulting loss to our privacy is likely to be permanent. In *Kyllo*, the Supreme Court concluded that the use of an advanced thermal detection device that allowed the police to detect heat emanating from marijuana plants growing inside the defendant's home constituted a "search" for the purposes of the Fourth Amendment and was presumptively unreasonable without a warrant. The Court placed great weight on the fact that the device was new, "not in general public use," and had been used to "explore details of a private home that would previously have been unknowable without physical intrusion." Implicit in the Court's holding is the principle that once a technology is in general public use and its capabilities are known, a reasonable expectation of privacy under the Fourth Amendment may no longer attach.

Several of the Act's enhanced surveillance tools, and the civil liberties concerns they raise, are examined below.

Sneak and peek searches

Section 213 of the Act authorizes federal agents to conduct "sneak and peek searches," or covert searches of a person's home or office that are conducted without notifying the person of the execution of the search warrant until after the search has been completed. Section 213 authorizes delayed notice of the execution of a search warrant upon a showing of "reasonable cause to believe that providing immediate notification . . . may have an adverse result." Section 213 also authorizes the delay of notice of the execution of a warrant to conduct a seizure of items where the court finds a "reasonable necessity" for the seizure.

Section 213 contravenes the "common law 'knock and announce' principle," which forms an essential part of the Fourth Amendment's reasonableness inquiry. When notice of a search is delayed, one is foreclosed from pointing out deficiencies in the warrant to the officer executing it, and from monitoring whether the search is being conducted in accordance with the warrant. In addition, Section 213, by authorizing delayed notice of the execution of a warrant to conduct a seizure of items, contravenes Rule 41(d) of the Federal Rules of Criminal Procedure, which requires that, "The officer taking property under the warrant shall give to the person from whom or from whose premises the property was taken a copy of the warrant and a receipt for the property taken or shall leave the copy and receipt at the place from which the property was taken."

Under Section 213, notice may be delayed for a "reasonable period." Already, DOJ has staked out its position that a "reasonable period" can be considerably longer than the seven days authorized by the Second Circuit Court of Appeals in *United States v. Villegas*, and by the Ninth Circuit Court of Appeals in *United States v. Freitas*. DOJ states in its *Field Guidance on New Authorities (Redacted) Enacted in the 2001 Anti-Terrorism Legislation* that "[a]nalogy to other statutes suggest [*sic*] that the period of delay could be substantial if circumstances warrant," and cites in support of this proposition a case that found a 90-day delay in providing notice of a wiretap warrant to constitute "a reasonable time." Notably, Section 213 is not limited to terrorism investigations, but extends to all criminal investigations, and is not scheduled to expire.

Access to records in international investigations

Section 215 is one of several provisions in the USA PATRIOT Act that relaxes the requirements, and extends the reach, of the Foreign Intelligence Surveillance Act of 1978 (FISA). Under Section 215, the Director of the FBI or a designee as low in rank as an Assistant Special Agent in Charge may apply for a court order requiring the production of "any tangible things (including books, records, papers, documents, and other items)" upon his written statement that these items are being sought for an investigation "to protect against international terrorism or clandestine intelligence activities." A judge presented with an application under Section 215 is required to enter an order if he "finds that the application meets the requirements of this section."

Notably absent from Section 215 is the restriction in the FISA provision it amends that had required the government to specify in its application for a court order that "there are specific and articulable facts giving reason to believe that the person to whom the records pertain is a foreign power or an agent of a foreign power." Now, under Section 215, the FBI may obtain sensitive personal records by simply certifying that they are sought for an investigation "to protect against international terrorism or clandestine intelligence activities." The FBI need not suspect the person whose records are being sought of any wrongdoing. Furthermore, the class of persons whose records are obtainable under Section 215 is no longer limited to foreign powers and their agents, but may include United States citizens and lawful permanent residents, or "United States persons" in the parlance of the FISA. While Section 215 bars investigations of United States persons "solely upon the basis of activities protected by the first amendment to the Constitution," it does nothing to bar investigations based on other activities that tie them, no matter how loosely, to an international terrorism investigation. . . .

Evading the Fourth Amendment

Perhaps the most radical provision of the USA PATRIOT Act is Section 218, which amends FISA's wiretap and physical search provisions. Under FISA, court orders permitting the executive to conduct surreptitious foreign intelligence wiretaps and physical searches may be obtained without the showing of probable cause required for wiretaps and physical searches in criminal investigations. Until the enactment of the Act, orders issued under FISA's lax standards were restricted to situations where the gathering of foreign intelligence information was "*the* purpose" of the surveillance.

Under Section 218, however, orders may be issued under FISA's lax standards where the primary purpose of the surveillance is criminal investigation, and the gathering of foreign intelligence information constitutes only "a *significant* purpose"of the surveillance. As a result, Section

218 allows law enforcement agencies conducting a criminal investigation to circumvent the Fourth Amendment whenever they are able to claim that the gathering of foreign intelligence constitutes "a significant purpose." In doing so, Section 218 gives the FBI a green light to resume domestic spying on government "enemies"—a program that reached an ugly apex under J. Edgar Hoover's directorship.

In the seminal case of *United States v. United States District Court for the Eastern District of Michigan (Keith)*, the Supreme Court rejected President Richard Nixon's ambitious bid for the unchecked executive power to conduct warrantless wiretaps when investigating national security threats posed by *domestic* groups with no foreign ties. The Court recognized that national security cases reflect "a convergence of First and Fourth Amendment values not present in cases of 'ordinary' crime." With respect to the First Amendment, the Court wisely observed that "[o]fficial surveillance, whether its purpose be criminal investigation or ongoing intelligence gathering, risks infringement of constitutionally protected privacy of speech" because of "the inherent vagueness of the domestic security concept . . . and the temptation to utilize such surveillances to oversee political dissent."

[The PATRIOT] Act authorizes federal agents to conduct "sneak and peek searches," or covert searches of a person's home or office that are conducted without notifying the person.

With respect to the Fourth Amendment, the Court acknowledged the constitutional basis for the President's domestic security role, but refused to exempt the President from the Fourth Amendment's warrant requirement. The Court explained that the oversight function assumed by the judiciary in its review of applications for warrants "accords with our basic constitutional doctrine that individual freedoms will best be preserved through a separation of powers and division of functions among the different branches and levels of Government."

Notably, the *Keith* Court declined to examine "the scope of the President's surveillance power with respect to the activities of *foreign* powers, within or without this country." To fill the vacuum left in the wake of the *Keith* decision, in 1978 Congress enacted FISA, which is premised on the assumption that Fourth Amendment safeguards are not as critical in foreign intelligence investigations as they are in criminal investigations. The Supreme Court has yet to rule on FISA's constitutionality. However, both the Fourth and Ninth Circuits have cautioned that applying FISA's lax standards to criminal investigations raises serious Fourth Amendment concerns. In *United States v. Truong Dinh Hung*, the Fourth Circuit held that "the executive should be excused from securing a warrant only when the surveillance is conducted '*primarily*' for foreign intelligence reasons," because "once surveillance becomes *primarily a criminal investigation*, the courts are entirely competent to make the usual probable cause determination, and because, importantly, individual privacy interests come to the fore and government foreign policy concerns recede when the government is primarily attempting to form the basis for a criminal prosecution." In a similar vein, the Ninth Circuit held in *United States v. Johnson* that "the investigation of criminal activity cannot be the primary purpose of [FISA] surveillance" and that "[FISA] is not to be used as an end-run around the Fourth Amendment's prohibition of warrantless searches."

The constitutionality of Section 218 is in considerable doubt. The extremist position staked out by DOJ in the Bryant Letter, which argues that "[i]f the government's heightened interest in self-defense justifies the use of deadly force, then it certainly would also justify warrantless searches," would undermine the separation of powers doctrine. Until the Supreme Court weighs in on this matter, the government will find itself in a quandary each time it seeks to prosecute a criminal defendant based on evidence that, although properly obtained under the lesser showing required by Section 218, does not meet the probable cause showing required by the Fourth Amendment. Should the government decide to base prosecutions on such evidence, it will run the risk that the evidence will be suppressed under the Fourth Amendment exclusionary rule. Section 218 is scheduled to expire on December 31, 2005.

Sharing of sensitive information

Section 203 of the USA PATRIOT Act authorizes the disclosure, without judicial supervision, of certain criminal and foreign intelligence information to officials of the FBI, CIA, and INS, as well as other federal agencies, where receipt of the information will "assist the official . . . in the performance of his official duties." Section 203(a) permits the disclosure of matters occurring before a grand jury—a category that is as boundless in scope as the powers of a grand jury to subpoena records and witnesses. Section 203(b) permits the disclosure of recordings of intercepted telephone and Internet conversations. And Section 203(d) permits the disclosure of foreign intelligence obtained as part of a criminal investigation.

While some additional sharing of information between agencies is undoubtedly appropriate given the nature of the terrorist threats we face, the Act fails to protect us from the dangers posed to our political freedoms and our privacy when sensitive personal information is widely shared without court supervision. A cautionary tale can be found in the 1976 report of the Senate's Church Committee, which revealed that the FBI and CIA had spied on thousands of law-abiding citizens, from civil rights workers to anti-Vietnam War protestors, who had been targeted solely because they were believed to harbor politically dissident views. Section 203(a) is not scheduled to expire. Subsections (b) and (d) of Section 203, however, are scheduled to expire.

Stripping immigrants of constitutional protections

The USA PATRIOT Act deprives immigrants of their due process and First Amendment rights through two mechanisms that operate in tandem. First, Section 411 vastly expands the class of immigrants who are subject to removal on terrorism grounds through its broad definitions of the terms "terrorist activity," "engage in terrorist activity," and "terrorist organization." Second, Section 412 vastly expands the authority of the Attorney General to place immigrants he suspects are engaged in terrorist activities in detention while their removal proceedings are pending.

Section 411 vastly expands the class of immigrants that can be removed on terrorism grounds. The term "terrorist activity" is commonly understood to be limited to pre-meditated and politically-motivated violence targeted against a civilian population. Section 411, however, stretches the term beyond recognition to encompass any crime that involves the use of a "weapon or dangerous device (other than for mere personal monetary gain)." Under this broad definition, an immigrant who grabs a knife or makeshift weapon in the midst of a heat-of-the-moment altercation or in committing a crime of passion may be subject to removal as a "terrorist."

The [PATRIOT] Act fails to protect us from the dangers posed to our political freedoms and our privacy when sensitive personal information is widely shared without court supervision.

The term "engage in terrorist activity" has also been expanded to include soliciting funds for, soliciting membership for, and providing material support to, a "terrorist organization," even when that organization has legitimate political and humanitarian ends and the non-citizen seeks only to support these lawful ends. In such situations, Section 411 would permit guilt to be imposed solely on the basis of political associations protected by the First Amendment.

To complicate matters further, the term "terrorist organization" is no longer limited to organizations that have been officially designated as terrorist and that therefore have had their designations published in the Federal Register for all to see. Instead, Section 411 now includes as "terrorist organizations" groups that have never been designated as terrorist if they fall under the loose criterion of "two or more individuals, whether organized or not," which engage in specified terrorist activities. In situations where a non-citizen has solicited funds for, solicited membership for, or provided material support to, an undesignated "terrorist organization," Section 411 saddles him with the difficult, if not impossible, burden of "demonstrat[ing] that he did not know, and should not reasonably have known, that the act would further the organization's terrorist activity."...

Detention at the attorney general's decree

At the same time that Section 411 vastly expands the class of immigrants who are removable on terrorist grounds, Section 412 vastly inflates the Attorney General's power to detain immigrants who are suspected of falling into that class. Upon no more than the Attorney General's unreviewed certification that he has "reasonable grounds to believe" that a non-citizen is engaged in terrorist activities or other activities that threaten the national security, a non-citizen can be detained for as long as seven days without being charged with either a criminal or immigration violation. This low level of suspicion falls far short of a finding of probable cause, and appears even to fall short of the "reasonable and articulable suspicion" that supports a brief investigatory stop under the Fourth Amendment. . . .

The [PATRIOT] Act will deprive non-citizens of their liberty without due process of law.

The Due Process Clause "applies to all 'persons' within the United States, including aliens, whether their presence is lawful, unlawful, temporary, or permanent." Yet, Section 412 exposes immigrants to extended, and, in some cases, indefinite, detention on the sole authority of the Attorney General's untested certification that he has "reasonable grounds to believe" that a non-citizen is engaged in terrorist activities. It remains to be seen what evidentiary safeguards, if any, the Attorney General will build into his regulations implementing Section 412. . . . Nevertheless, it is hard to avoid the conclusion that the Act will deprive non-citizens of their liberty without due process of law.

In short, immigrants who engage in political activities in connection with any organization that has ever violated the law risk being certified as terrorists, placed in mandatory detention, and removed, whether on a technical immigration violation or on terrorism grounds. . . .

Uphold the Bill of Rights

Our commitment to the Bill of Rights and to the democratic values that define this nation has been put to the test by the events of September 11. Already, Congress and the Administration have demonstrated their eagerness to sacrifice civil liberties in hopes of gaining an added measure of security. The task of upholding the Bill of Rights—or acquiescing in its surrender—will soon fall to the judiciary, as lawsuits testing the constitutionality of the USA PATRIOT Act wind their way through the courts.

In what we have come to regard as some of the most shameful episodes in our history, the judiciary has consistently bowed to the wishes of the political branches of government in times of crisis by finding the state interest in national security to be paramount to all competing interests. During World War I, the Supreme Court upheld the conviction of socialist Eugene Debs for expressing his opposition to World War I, refusing to recognize his non-violent, anti-war advocacy as speech protected by the First Amendment. More recently, following the bombing of Pearl Harbor during World War II, the Supreme Court upheld an Executive Order mandating the internment of more than 100,000 Japanese-Americans and Japanese immigrants based solely on their ancestry, refusing to recognize their preventive detention as a violation of the Equal Protection Clause.

The extent to which the judiciary will defer to the Administration's views on the troubling First and Fourth Amendment issues presented by the USA PATRIOT Act, will tolerate ethnic and ideological profiling by the Administration as it implements the Act, and will allow the due process rights of immigrants in detention to be eroded remains to be seen. Certainly, the more anxious the times become, the more likely the judiciary will be to side with the Administration—at least where judges are convinced that the measures are vital to the national security, are not motivated by discriminatory intent, and tread as lightly as possible upon civil liberties. The recent words of Supreme Court Justice Sandra Day O'Connor, who so often figures as the swing vote on pivotal decisions, do not hold out hope for a vigorous defense of our political freedoms by the judiciary. Following a visit to Ground Zero, where the World Trade Centers once stood, the Justice bleakly predicted, "We're likely to experience more restrictions on personal freedom than has ever been the case in this country."

5

The Department of Homeland Security Will Protect Americans Against Terrorists

George W. Bush

President George W. Bush took office on January 20, 2001.

The new Department of Homeland Security, which consolidates dozens of federal agencies within one Cabinet-level organization, will ensure that America's homeland security efforts are comprehensive and coordinated. The new department will analyze intelligence collected by the FBI, CIA, and the National Security Agency; it will coordinate the nation's efforts to combat cyberterrorism and weapons of mass destruction; it will coordinate with state and local governments on homeland security issues; and the new department will eliminate much of the redundancy and overlapping responsibilities that have traditionally characterized U.S. counter-terrorism efforts.

Editor's note: President Bush issued the following remarks on November 25, 2002, at the signing of the Homeland Security Act.

Today, we are taking historic action to defend the United States and protect our citizens against the dangers of a new era. With my signature, this act of Congress will create a new Department of Homeland Security, ensuring that our efforts to defend this country are comprehensive and united.

The new department will analyze threats, will guard our borders and airports, protect our critical infrastructure, and coordinate the response of our nation for future emergencies. The Department of Homeland Security will focus the full resources of the American government on the safety of the American people. This essential reform was carefully considered by

George W. Bush, "President Bush Signs Homeland Security Act," www.whitehouse.gov, November 25, 2002.

Congress and enacted with strong bipartisan majorities. . . .

From the morning of September the 11th, 2001, to this hour, America has been engaged in an unprecedented effort to defend our freedom and our security. We're fighting a war against terror with all our resources, and we're determined to win.

Dozens of agencies charged with homeland security will now be located within one Cabinet department with the mandate and legal authority to protect our people.

With the help of many nations, with the help of 90 nations, we're tracking terrorist activity, we're freezing terrorist finances, we're disrupting terrorist plots, we're shutting down terrorist camps, we're on the hunt one person at a time. Many terrorists are now being interrogated. Many terrorists have been killed. We've liberated a country.

We recognize our greatest security is found in the relentless pursuit of these cold-blooded killers. Yet, because terrorists are targeting America, the front of the new war is here in America. Our life changed and changed in dramatic fashion on September the 11th, 2001.

In the last 14 months, every level of our government has taken steps to be better prepared against a terrorist attack. We understand the nature of the enemy. We understand they hate us because of what we love. We're doing everything we can to enhance security at our airports and power plants and border crossings. We've deployed detection equipment to look for weapons of mass destruction. We've given law enforcement better tools to detect and disrupt terrorist cells which might be hiding in our own country.

And through separate legislation I signed earlier today [November 25, 2002], we will strengthen security at our nation's 361 seaports, adding port security agents, requiring ships to provide more information about the cargo, crew and passengers they carry. And I want to thank the members of Congress for working hard on this important piece of legislation as well.

A unified response

The Homeland Security Act of 2002 takes the next critical steps in defending our country. The continuing threat of terrorism, the threat of mass murder on our own soil will be met with a unified, effective response.

Dozens of agencies charged with homeland security will now be located within one Cabinet department with the mandate and legal authority to protect our people. America will be better able to respond to any future attacks, to reduce our vulnerability and, most important, prevent the terrorists from taking innocent American lives.

The Department of Homeland Security will have nearly 170,000 employees, dedicated professionals who will wake up each morning with the overriding duty of protecting their fellow citizens. As federal workers, they have rights, and those rights will be fully protected. And I'm grateful that the Congress listened to my concerns and retained the authority of the President to put the right people in the right place at the right time in the defense of our country.

I've great confidence in the men and women who will serve in this department and in the man I've asked to lead it. As I prepare to sign this bill into law, I am pleased to announce that I will nominate Governor Tom Ridge as our nation's first Secretary of Homeland Security. (Applause.)

Americans know Tom as an experienced public servant and as the leader of our homeland security efforts since last year. Tom accepted that assignment in urgent circumstances, resigning as the governor of Pennsylvania to organize the White House Office of Homeland Security and to develop a comprehensive strategy to protect the American people. He's done a superb job. He's the right man for this new and great responsibility. (Applause.)

We're going to put together a fine team to work with Tom. The Secretary of the Navy, Gordon England, will be nominated for the post of Deputy Secretary. (Applause.)

And Asa Hutchinson of Arkansas, now the Administrator of the Drug Enforcement Administration, will be nominated to serve as Under Secretary for Border and Transportation Security. (Applause.)

This new department will analyze intelligence information on terror threats collected by the CIA, the FBI, the National Security Agency and others.

The Secretary-designate and his team have an immense task ahead of them. Setting up the Department of Homeland Security will involve the most extensive reorganization of the federal government since Harry Truman signed the National Security Act. To succeed in their mission, leaders of the new department must change the culture of many diverse agencies—directing all of them toward the principal objective of protecting the American people. The effort will take time, and focus, and steady resolve. It will also require full support from both the administration and the Congress. Adjustments will be needed along the way. Yet this is pressing business, and the hard work of building a new department begins today.

When the Department of Homeland Security is fully operational, it will enhance the safety of our people in very practical ways.

A comprehensive strategy

First, this new department will analyze intelligence information on terror threats collected by the CIA, the FBI, the National Security Agency and others. The department will match this intelligence against the nation's vulnerabilities—and work with other agencies, and the private sector, and state and local governments to harden America's defenses against terror.

Second, the department will gather and focus all our efforts to face the challenge of cyberterrorism, and the even worse danger of nuclear, chemical, and biological terrorism. This department will be charged with encouraging research on new technologies that can detect these threats in time to prevent an attack.

Third, state and local governments will be able to turn for help and information to one federal domestic security agency, instead of more than 20 agencies that currently divide these responsibilities. This will help our local governments work in concert with the federal government for the sake of all the people of America.

Fourth, the new department will bring together the agencies responsible for border, coastline, and transportation security. There will be a coordinated effort to safeguard our transportation systems and to secure the border so that we're better able to protect our citizens and welcome our friends.

Fifth, the department will work with state and local officials to prepare our response to any future terrorist attack that may come. We have found that the first hours and even the first minutes after the attack can be crucial in saving lives, and our first responders need the carefully planned and drilled strategies that will make their work effective.

The Department of Homeland Security will also end a great deal of duplication and overlapping responsibilities. Our objective is to spend less on administrators in offices and more on working agents in the field—less on overhead and more on protecting our neighborhoods and borders and waters and skies from terrorists.

With a vast nation to defend, we can neither predict nor prevent every conceivable attack. And in a free and open society, no department of government can completely guarantee our safety against ruthless killers, who move and plot in shadows. Yet our government will take every possible measure to safeguard our country and our people.

We're fighting a new kind of war against determined enemies. And public servants long into the future will bear the responsibility to defend Americans against terror. This administration and this Congress have the duty of putting that system into place. We will fulfill that duty. With the Homeland Security Act, we're doing everything we can to protect America. We're showing the resolve of this great nation to defend our freedom, our security and our way of life.

It's now my privilege to sign the Homeland Security Act of 2002. (Applause.)

6

The Department of Homeland Security May Make Americans Less Safe

Eric R. Taylor

Eric R. Taylor served in the Chemical Corps of the U.S. Army and is now an associate professor of chemistry at the University of Louisiana at Lafayette.

A Department of Homeland Security (DHS) has been proposed to address the lack of inter-agency cooperation among the FBI, CIA, National Security Agency (NSA), Immigration and Naturalization Service, and other agencies that, prior to the September 11, 2001, terrorist attacks had fragmented U.S. counter-terrorism efforts. The fundamental problem with a new Department of Homeland Security (DHS)—and its predecessor, the Office of Homeland Security—is that it lacks the authority to fulfill its mission. The department would consolidate dozens of federal agencies, but not the FBI, CIA, or the NSA. Thus, inter-agency "turf battles" and lack of effective cooperation would likely continue much as it had without the DHS. The DHS resembles a bureaucratic clone of the NSA, so it is unclear why the NSA could not have been charged with the DHS's new responsibilities. Ultimately, the creation of the DHS will serve to make homeland security efforts more bureaucratic, sluggish, and less effective.

Editor's note: The following viewpoint was written in June 2002, when the Homeland Security Act, which established the Department of Homeland Security in November 2002, was still being debated in Congress. Taylor makes frequent reference to the Office of Homeland Security (OHS), the White House office established prior to the Cabinet-level Department of Homeland Security.

The terrorist attack on September 11, 2001, was an epochal event in U.S. history and stimulated a dramatic change in U.S. policy toward terrorism at home and abroad. As Americans united in self-defense and braced for a protracted war, the White House created the Office of Homeland Security and the Homeland Security Council to coordinate and oversee the efforts against terrorism of all federal departments and agencies. The Bush administration proposes to double the budget for homeland security to $38 billion.

The challenge before the OHS director is no small one. The mission of the OHS is to develop and coordinate the implementation of a comprehensive national strategy to secure the United States from terrorist threats or attacks. The office coordinates the executive branch's efforts to detect, prepare for, prevent, protect against, respond to, and recover from terrorist attacks within the United States.

Insufficient authority

The OHS is essentially an adaptation of a proposed cabinet-level national homeland security agency, originally recommended by the congressionally mandated U.S. Commission on National Security/21st Century. To compound the organizational complexity, in parallel with OHS, President [George W.] Bush recently proposed a department that would have the same legal standing and authority as any other cabinet department. The OHS, however, has no authority to enforce implementation of its plans.

Nonetheless, the creation of the office may serve to spotlight the problems that have hampered past efforts to integrate federal departments and agencies into a unified front for homeland defense. The core problems include legal constraints on what such government entities can do and the multitude of departments and agencies—each claiming a unique, if not premier, role—involved in fighting terrorism. The State Department, the Defense Department, and the Justice Department and its Federal Bureau of Investigation justify their involvement by their prominent role in the security function of the federal government. Some cabinet departments opposed the creation of the OHS altogether. Turf battles have become the institutional practice of all agencies and departments and rest, in part on internal secrecy policies. The agencies are unwilling to disclose intelligence to outside interests—a process called "stovepiping." Those concerns have been significant impediments to federal preparedness efforts for years.

The new cabinet department will have authority over the parts of agencies subsumed under it but not over the many more that remain outside its fiefdom.

It remains to be seen just how successful any new cabinet department will be in overcoming those entrenched practices.

The one promise embodied in the OHS is a single head who has titular, if not sole, responsibility for the government's efforts against terrorism. But the OHS has no constitutional or statutory authority over the heads of other cabinet departments and independent agencies. In reality, the OHS director is not part of the critical chain of command; he is more of an aide-de-camp. The other department heads know the limitations of his office.

The new cabinet department will have authority over the parts of agencies subsumed under it but not over the many more that remain outside its fiefdom. Surrogates aside, the president remains the sole executive branch official responsible and accountable to the nation for its security, or lack thereof.

In the lengthy list of responsibilities of the OHS, as set forth in the executive order creating it, a single phrase occurs five times: "The Office shall work with Federal, State, and local agencies. . . . Historically, interagency cooperation has been stymied by the secrecy maintained by departments and agencies and their vigorous protection of their own constitutional and statutory mandates. To collaborate with another department or agency seemed a tacit admission that the agency in question was deficient in meeting its responsibilities and needed outside help. Furthermore, in the federal view, valid or not, state and local agencies generally fail to meet the operational standards and abilities of federal agencies. Those intrinsic impediments to cooperation among agencies will not be removed by creating an impotent OHS that is powerless to mandate such coordination. The new cabinet secretary can coordinate activities within the new department, but much of the federal effort remains outside his jurisdiction.

Section 5 of the executive order also establishes the Homeland Security Council, which is the domestic counterpart of the National Security Council. According to the order, the HSC "shall serve as the mechanism for ensuring coordination of homeland security-related activities of executive departments and agencies and effective development and implementation of homeland security policies." Not surprisingly, the composition of the HSC reads like a carbon copy of the NSC.

Homeland security vs. national security

The similar compositions and responsibilities of the HSC and the NSC raise the question, What is the real difference between national security and homeland security? It seems to be a matter of semantics—and perhaps of the natural political propensity of governmental institutions to grow in size. To the bureaucratic mind, each problem seems to require a dedicated office. Why the NSC could not have shouldered the responsibility to lead the government's efforts against terrorism from the outset is a mystery. If terrorism is a homeland security threat, it is also a national security threat.

Unlike the HSC, the NSC is a statutorily empowered agency. Virtually all of the tools and authority not vested in the HSC and the OHS are already formally installed in the NSC and the national security adviser. The national security adviser has access to intelligence from overseas that the OHS does not have. The OHS has access only to information that is collected by law enforcement agencies domestically. The new cabinet agency will have an intelligence analysis office that seems to duplicate that of the intelligence community and some agencies within it, perhaps exacerbating the problem of information sharing among the already too numerous agencies of that community.

The NSC would have been the logical central coordinator of anti-terrorism efforts, which would dovetail with its other national security concerns and responsibilities. According to the White House's description of the functions of the NSC, "The National Security Council is the President's principal forum for considering national security and foreign policy matters with his senior national security advisors and cabinet officials. . . . The Council also serves as the President's principal arm for coordinating these policies among various government agencies." Coordination of national security-related policy matters is already one of the responsibilities of the NSC.

The regular members of the NSC are the president; the vice president; the secretaries of State, Treasury, and Defense; and the assistant to the president for national security affairs. Also serving as advisers to the council are the chairman of the Joint Chiefs of Staff and the director of central intelligence. The president may invite any other senior members of the executive branch to attend meetings if matters before the council involve their areas of responsibility. Essentially, an expanded organizational chart of the NSC could include the heads of all cabinet and independent agencies that have a role in combating terrorism. That group of agencies is the same as the group represented on the HSC.

Added bureaucracies will only cause agile terrorist groups glee as they outmaneuver sluggish government attempts to counter them.

The asserted purpose of the HSC is to be a domestic counterpart to the NSC. But in terrorism, as shown by the attacks of September 11, the demarcation between domestic and foreign can be a lethal contrivance. The HSC is to assume exclusive charge of terrorism matters, but what part of the HSC's role in terrorism and homeland security could not have been better fulfilled by the NSC? The HSC to be seems essentially a bureaucratic clone of the NSC, but the HSC is responsible for only the government's efforts against terrorism. The NSC fundamentally is and always has been the nucleus of what is currently the function of the duplicative HSC.

In addition to the HSC, there is the new Transportation Security Administration, which has jurisdiction over all transportation security matters, including air travel security. The government has metastasized again, this time in the name of fighting terrorism. The proliferation of government entities does not streamline response coordination, much less response implementation, in the event of a serious terrorist attack.

Although increased sharing of intelligence across agencies may be necessary in some, if not all, cases, "stovepiping" is not the only problem. Removing departmental and subordinate agency obstacles to interagency cooperation is not a panacea. Inventing, repackaging, merging, or cloning agencies in a modern-day version of circling the nation's wagons will not solve the fundamental operational problem. The president must direct priorities, demand cooperation, and command implementation. His leadership and orders can further the needed coordination and integration of government efforts far more than can the OHS director, who has no authority over the department secretaries and agency heads. After all, Tom Ridge [who was appointed head of the OHS and later the Department of Homeland Security] brings no technical expertise or experience in homeland security to the table.

Although the OHS and the HSC are surprisingly open to public view, the NSC would seem to be the logical place to vest the coordination and implementation of homeland security—particularly the integration of those efforts with other national security concerns under the seamless command that only the president can provide. The OHS and the HSC seem to be an ad hoc and unnecessary duplication, and the director appears to be a powerless surrogate. Absent statutory authority, the OHS has no fangs. The office must address many problems, not the least of which is its own operational impotence. The heads of powerful cabinet departments will be more likely to ignore what the OHS says if it does not have statutory authority. Creating a cabinet-level Department of Homeland Security will probably require the creation of a new central bureaucracy to control the disparate agencies brought together to form the new department.

After World War II, the merging of the War and Navy Departments resulted in the creation of an Office of the Secretary of Defense to manage the new Department of Defense. More important, creating new bureaucracies is questionable when the existing NSC and national security adviser should naturally have terrorism within their purview.

So why do we need a dedicated OHS and HSC, a new cabinet-level Department of Homeland Security, and numerous other lesser new agencies? What is different now? More laws and more agencies with competing interests exist now than did before September 11. More money is being poured into homeland security, which is nothing more than national defense by a new name. Whatever institutional deficiencies existed before September 11 remain. Is the creation of the department, the OHS, and the HSC an admission that the NSC and others have failed? Is the U.S. government facing a serious public relations problem in the wake of massive deaths at the hands of terrorists? The government's apparent solution: change the name and repackage the product. But the same people are at the helm with the same mindset—that bigger government and more money will solve the problem. Added bureaucracies will only cause agile terrorist groups glee as they outmaneuver sluggish government attempts to counter them. A more streamlined government and an educated public could more efficiently and less chaotically respond to the terrorist threat.

Public education: the bedrock of our democracy and homeland defense

In January 2002 Ridge said, "Homeland security begins in your hometown." Logically, that must mean security also begins with the public. For the public to respond to an alert, it needs to know what to watch for. In light of the anthrax attacks [that occurred in fall 2001] and concern about future strikes using weapons of mass destruction, some education of the public about terrorism is required.

A cardinal principle of emergency management is education of the public about natural and technological disasters. Educating the public also garners its support for government action in a crisis. Moreover, citizens educated about weapons of mass destruction can assist government during alerts—the public would know what it was looking for, what to do, and how to respond. If, as CIA director George Tenet has publicly told Congress, the United States is still very much at risk of harm from al-Qaeda [the terrorist network responsible for the September 11 attacks] for the foreseeable future, then government has a legal and moral obligation to inform the public. It needs to provide specific information on what the threats are, how to recognize them, what to do, and how people can individually protect and minimize harm to themselves, as well as meaningfully help the government.

Nebulous alerts from OHS provided cover for federal officials still reeling from criticism that they did not provide advance warning of the September 11 attacks, but they did nothing for the public except cause alarm. In fact, when repeated, they take on the air of crying wolf.

The OHS came up with a coding system with five colors to differentiate various alert levels. The alert levels range from green—low risk of terrorist threats—to red—severe risk of terrorist attacks—but still provide only vague guidance about what measures state and local communities should take. Security would be enhanced by more specific guidance.

The American people are not drones who cannot, should not, or need not know what the potential dangers are. The public shares the risks of terrorism and should be privy to knowledge about the threats.

The Federal Emergency Management Agency (which will be folded into the new cabinet department), the agency with jurisdiction over such public training, is doing an insufficient job. FEMA's Introductory Management Course emphasizes that the education of the public is a key element in any emergency preparedness plan: "Remember, citizens should be given all the information they need to know in order to plan their response to disasters and to instill confidence in the plan" and "don't wait until a disaster strikes before you tell the people what to do. Your motto should be the same as the scouts. You want the people to BE PREPARED." But, in practice, the agency has no single, comprehensive, nontechnical source of official information to prepare the public to respond to a nuclear, biological, or chemical attack by terrorists. FEMA does offer a misnamed self-study course titled "Emergency Response to Terrorism." The course curriculum provides good information about the threats, but not about protective measures that the public could take if an attack occurs.

FEMA should enhance its training of the public, but that in no way requires homeland security to fall under the jurisdiction of an entirely new department. Also, FEMA could provide the training under the overall direction of the NSC and the national security adviser just as well as it could under the HSC and the OHS.

The problem of information sharing remains

The attack on September 11 revealed deficiencies in our intelligence gathering and analysis mechanisms and laid bare the entrenched inter- as well as intradepartmental coordination problems endemic to the federal bureaucracy. Removing those systemic impediments will require more than the usual incremental reforms. The OHS, lacking statutory authority and budgetary power, is not equipped to accomplish that mission. The only power the office possesses to implement change is the power of persuasion—convincing the multitude of department and agency heads, who have neither the statutory obligation nor incentives to comply with OHS desires, to cooperate. Creating a new cabinet-level agency does nothing to solve the original problem of information sharing among agencies outside its purview—for example, the FBI and CIA.

Creating a new cabinet-level agency does nothing to solve the original problem of information sharing among agencies outside its purview.

The establishment of the OHS, the HSC, and the planned cabinet department are well intentioned and perhaps reassuring to the public. However, their very existence would seem to hinder, rather than expedite, coordination and implementation of homeland security efforts by creating yet other layers of bureaucracy. Also, the HSC is merely a carbon copy of the NSC. The NSC's statutory responsibilities and authority would appear to logically and automatically include homeland security—a component of national security. The real core issue in homeland security is complete, accurate, and timely intelligence, to which the NSC already has full access. Access to and analysis and dissemination of intelligence, as well as policy implementation based on that information, are central to NSC functions. The OHS, on the other hand, has only limited access to intelligence and is powerless to compel implementation of its plans. The cabinet department will have an office for analyzing intelligence that appears to be redundant with that of the intelligence community and some of its agencies (for example, the CIA and FBI) and may exacerbate the original problem—that of lack of intelligence sharing.

To achieve real improvements in homeland security, not politically symbolic ones, accountability and reform are vital. They can be realized only in an organization and an individual who have access to all intelligence and the president and have the constitutional or statutory authority to command action. Those criteria point to the NSC. If any agency should have seen the attacks of September 11 coming, the NSC certainly should have. Reform of its mission, role, and authority is paramount to efforts to improve coordination and implementation of plans to combat terrorism. For seamless supervision of coordination and implementation of policy, homeland security can be integrated within the NSC's overall national security responsibilities. New bureaucracies created during a national crisis and grafted artificially onto existing bureaucratic structures cannot resolve the problems that the September 11 attacks have dramatically highlighted.

7

The Government Should Abandon the Total Information Awareness Project

James M. Wall

James M. Wall is senior contributing editor of the Christian Century.

The Total Information Awareness (TIA) system is a Department of Defense project that aims to collect and integrate information that is stored in countless government databases throughout the country. Ultimately TIA could result in the government having the ability to obtain detailed personal information on every American. Through sophisticated data mining techniques, the government would be able to track credit card purchases, travel records, telephone calls, e-mail messages, and other information in order to compile a profile on an individual that indicates whether he or she might be involved in terrorism. This would constitute a gross violation of civil liberties and an abuse of governmental power.

How does one express appropriate outrage over the Defense Department's Total Information Awareness program? Start by invoking the "Keep Pete Rose out of the Hall of Fame" principle:[1] sin can be forgiven, but it should not be honored. Yet Defense Secretary Donald Rumsfeld has honored sin and its legal twin—lying to Congress—by selecting former Irangate conspirator John Poindexter to direct the TIA. Poindexter will control a program that the Electronic Frontier Foundation describes as "a Defense Department project that . . . will effectively have wiretaps, dossiers, and tracking devices for every American citizen."

Poindexter escaped his jail term when a court ruled that he had testified while under immunity. Yet Georgetown University law professor Jonathan Turley describes the former U.S. Navy admiral as "the master ar-

---

1. Pete Rose, manager of the Cincinnati Reds, was accused of betting against his own team.

James M. Wall, "Eyes Are on You," *Christian Century*, vol. 120, January 11, 2003, p. 44. Copyright © 2003 by Christian Century Foundation. Reproduced by permission.

chitect behind the Iran-Contra scandal, the criminal conspiracy to sell arms to a terrorist nation, Iran, in order to surreptitiously fund an unlawful clandestine project in Nicaragua."

The program that Poindexter directs will identify, in the words of journalist Nat Hentoff, "suspicious patterns in your credit-card and bank data, medical records, the movies you click for on pay-per-view, passport applications, prescription purchases, e-mail messages, telephone calls, and anything you've done that winds up in court records, like divorces. Almost anything you do will leave a trace for these omnivorous computers, which will now contain records of your library book withdrawals, your loans and debts, and whatever you order by mail or on the Web."

As the antiwar movement in this country expands, both religious and secular opponents of war could fall under TIA's watchful eye.

The Defense Department's Web site describes the purpose of TIA: "to revolutionize the ability of the United States to detect, classify and identify foreign terrorists—and decipher their plans—and thereby enable the U.S. to take timely action to successfully preempt and defeat terrorist acts." According to Hentoff, the TIA started quietly, "without any official public notice, and without any congressional hearings." Funded by an initial appropriation of $200 million, the TIA will be able to "extensively mine government and commercial data banks, enabling the FBI, the CIA, and other intelligence agencies to collect information that will allow the government to essentially reconstruct the movements of citizens."

Monitoring citizens

Which citizens will be most closely scrutinized? At the moment, TIA is focusing on people who speak certain languages. TIA has a language identification program (officially called "Babylon") which focuses on Pashto, Dari (Afghan languages), Arabic and Mandarin. Given the national anxiety over terrorism, however, other languages will most likely be added. Korean speakers, for example, could become a target now that saber rattling has been heard from that corner, and Farsi (the Iranian language) cannot be far behind. Meanwhile, religion as a security benchmark is not mentioned by TIA, but the Washington war drum beaters have identified Islam as the religious belief system most closely identified with terrorism. Which leads to the assumption that as the antiwar movement in this country expands, both religious and secular opponents of war could fall under TIA's watchful eye.

On a recent trip to Tel Aviv [Israel], I was questioned by an Israeli security official who appeared reluctant to allow me into his country after he had identified me as an American journalist with a religious orientation. He asked: "What does your church believe is the actual location of the burial site of Jesus, the Church of the Holy Sepulcher or Gordon's Tomb?" I said my church had no strong feelings on that issue.

If I had embraced Gordon's Tomb as the preferred site, I might have counted as a Christian Zionist, since the more conservative Christian believers have a fondness for the quiet of Gordon's garden. The question, coming from one of the world's most experienced security-minded and terrorist-hunting organizations, did not seem relevant to security, but it did suggest that my questioner wanted to identify my particular Protestant orientation. Now he knows, and so does his data bank.

The TIA says its five-year goal is to achieve a "total reinvention of technologies for storing and accessing information . . . although database size will no longer be measured in the traditional sense, the amounts of data that will need to be stored and accessed will be unprecedented, measured in petabytes." The data bank will have help in gathering information. A Justice Department program that was proposed, then quickly dropped due to criticism, would have recruited mail carriers to watch for suspicious communication as frontline troops against terrorism. Terrorism strikes fear in the hearts of all people, which means that national fear could sanction other citizen frontline troops to spy on their neighbors.

If you don't speak Arabic, or if you are not a Muslim, or if you access only patriotic and morally uplifting Web sites, you may feel secure knowing that TIA is on the case, gathering information on suspicious people. This government intrusion may seem a small price to pay to prevent terrorist attacks. But we should remember the words German pastor Martin Niemoller said after spending seven years in [the Nazi death camp at] Dachau. "In Germany they came first for the communists, and I didn't speak up because I wasn't a communist." He went on to lament his failure to speak up for Jews, trade unionists and others, and concluded: "Then they came for me, and by that time there was no one left to speak up."

8

The Government Should Not Abandon the Total Information Awareness Project

Heather MacDonald

Heather MacDonald is a contributing editor at the Manhattan Institute's City Journal.

The almost hysterical backlash against the Pentagon's Total Information Awareness (TIA) project is unwarranted. The system would merely enable federal law enforcement agencies to better access information that the government *already has* in order to more effectively investigate and respond to terrorist threats. Critics of the program have exaggerated both its scope and intent, preying on Americans' fears of "Big Brother," the totalitarian government depicted in George Orwell's novel *1984*. The sensational claims made by many journalists about TIA are uninformed, misleading, and irresponsible. Facilitating law enforcement's access to government records is a sensible and important part of U.S. homeland security efforts.

E very week brings new evidence of al Qaeda's[1] continuing plots against the United States and the West. Yet the 108th Congress may well shut down one of the most promising efforts to preempt future attacks, thanks to a media misinformation blitz playing to Americans' outsized Big Brother[2] paranoia.

The Pentagon's prestigious research unit, the same Defense Advanced Research Projects Agency that helped invent the Internet, is exploring whether computers could detect terrorist planning activity by searching government and commercial databases across the globe. The program,

1. The al-Qaeda terrorist network was responsible for the September 11 attacks.   2. Big Brother is the name given to the totalitarian government in George Orwell's novel *1984*.

Heather MacDonald, "Total Misrepresentation: There's a Compelling Case to Be Made for the Pentagon's Total Information Awareness Program," *Weekly Standard*, vol. 8, January 27, 2003. Copyright © 2003 by News Corporation, Weekly Standard. Reproduced by permission.

dubbed Total Information Awareness (TIA), embodies the recognition that before an attack can take place, certain critical activities—casing targets, rehearsing, and procuring financing, supplies, and weapons—must occur, and that those activities will leave computer signatures. Had even a simple data-mining program been in place before [the September 11, 2001, terrorist attacks on America], a majority of the hijackers could have been identified. Remember that two of the 9/11 hijackers were already on a State Department watch list. When Khalid Almidhar and Nawaq Alhazmi bought their tickets on American Airlines Flight 77 in August, a search for people sharing addresses and frequent flier numbers with these al Qaeda operatives, as well as of their telephone contacts, would have uncovered over half the plotters.

Unwarranted hysteria

In early November [2002], both the *Washington Post* and the *New York Times* reported on the Total Information Awareness project without causing a ripple of concern. Then on November 14, *New York Times* pundit William Safire let fly with a column entitled "You Are a Suspect." He declared that "in the next few weeks," the government would compile a computer dossier on "every public and every private act of every American" unless TIA were stopped.

The media world uncorked the champagne bottles. Stories about the imminent advent of Big Brother rolled non-stop across television screens and newspaper editorial pages. In a typically garbled outburst of zeal, law professor Jonathan Turley wrote in the *Los Angeles Times*: "Long thought dead, it now appears that Orwell is busy at work in the darkest recesses of the Bush administration and its new Information Awareness Office." Politicians rushed to express their dismay and promised to defund this new Bush initiative to strip Americans of their freedom.

The TIA researchers are trying to teach computers to recognize suspicious patterns of activity . . . compiling dossiers on every American never enters the picture.

To call the Safire column and its progeny caricatures of the Pentagon project is too charitable. Their disconnection from reality was total. The notion that the program would result in "computer dossiers on 300 million Americans," as Safire exclaimed and dozens of editorialists echoed, is pure fiction. The TIA researchers are trying to teach computers to recognize suspicious patterns of activity in the billions of transactions that occur across the world daily; compiling dossiers on every American never enters the picture. The program—which is still at the stage—would start by mapping the personal networks of known terrorists and suspects, a traditional investigative technique merely given more juice by massive computing power. If John Doe placed several calls to [terrorist] Mohamed Atta before 9/11, that information would most certainly be stored for future reference, and any other of Mr. Doe's transactions with Islamic radicals would be flagged. His neighbor's purchase of golf clubs with a Visa card, on the other hand, would be invisible to the TIA computers.

Also left out of the nightmare scenarios are the numerous privacy protections being built into TIA. The program would sever names and other personal information from transactions. An analyst could query, for example, whether anyone had bought unusually large quantities of bomb-making chemicals and rented a large truck recently. The program might say yes, such a pattern had occurred, but it would not reveal the names of the people pursuing it unless the disclosure were approved by a judge or other legal authority. Like criminal investigators, analysts using TIA would be given access to private data only if their case for seeking it met certain legal standards. The program would also contain audit mechanisms automatically tracing where data are sent and who has seen them. Oversight would be built into the system. Policymakers should of course provide for criminal penalties for any abuses.

Equally specious has been the critics' personalizing of TIA as the devilish ambition of its director, Admiral John Poindexter. Poindexter was President [Ronald] Reagan's national security adviser and a lead player in the Iran-contra scandal.[3] Safire claims that "Poindexter is now realizing his 20-year dream: getting the data mining power to snoop on every public and private act of every American." Safire doesn't reveal how he knows what Poindexter has been dreaming for the last 20 years. Every privacy paranoiac has milked Poindexter's involvement in Iran-contra for all it's worth, and indeed, the Bush administration should have foreseen the ad hominem potential of his appointment. But the critics' charge that TIA represents Poindexter's personal desire to "monitor every aspect of your life," in the words of the *Atlanta Journal-Constitution*, is absurd. Should the technology prove feasible, Pentagon researchers would deliver it to law enforcement agencies like the FBI and the CIA to operate; Poindexter would have nothing to do with its implementation.

Specious arguments

The reaction to TIA is a textbook case of privacy hysteria. The Bush administration had better learn how to counter such outbreaks, for they will resurface with every new initiative to improve the country's intelligence capacity. They follow a predictable script:

• *Barely mention the motivation for the initiative, if at all.* Safire, like several of his followers, writes an entire column on TIA without once referring to terrorism or the 9/11 strikes.

• *Never, ever suggest an alternative.* Islamic terrorists wear no uniforms, carry no particular passport, and live inconspicuously among the target population for years. Many, sometimes all, of the steps leading up to an attack are legal; they become suspicious only when combined in a particular way in a particular context. TIA's critics adamantly oppose using data mining to detect suspicious patterns of activity in civilian populations, but they never propose an alternative method to find the terrorist enemy before he strikes.

---

3. The Iran-contra scandal was the criminal conspiracy to fund rebels in Nicaragua by selling arms to Iran.

• Remember the outcry after 9/11 over the intelligence community's failure to "connect the dots"? TIA is nothing other than a connect-the-dots tool, with a global scope that individual analysts cannot hope to match. Do its detractors simply hope that as the next attack nears, the same intelligence analysts who failed us last time, using the same inadequate tools, will get it right this time? They do not say.

Critics adamantly oppose using data mining to detect suspicious patterns of activity . . . but they never propose an alternative method to find the terrorist enemy before he strikes.

• *Assume the worst; ignore the best.* The *Kansas City Star* editorializes that if TIA proceeds, "Uncle Sam could end up listening to your phone conversations, reading your e-mail and monitoring your shopping trips." Well, yes, if defense intelligence analysts lose interest in al Qaeda and develop so strong a fascination with the quotidian affairs of John Q. Public that they are willing to risk their careers to abuse the system, that could happen. But the lawful use of TIA could also stop a smallpox release at Disneyland. TIA would allow investigators to identify, say, visa holders from terror-associated countries who had spent more than a month in Afghanistan during Taliban days[4] and who also shared addresses, phone numbers, or credit cards; it could spot airline ticket holders who had telephoned people on terror watch lists over the past year; and it could determine which visa applicants had traveled to certain cities contemporaneously with terrorist activity.

• *Use a privacy balancing test when pursuing your own interests, but demand privacy absolutism regarding the public good.* Americans are credit card junkies, cell phone aficionados, ATM devotees, and Internet shoppers. All of these consumer conveniences transfer vast swaths of personal information to corporations, which then often sell it for additional profit. Americans happily balance the privacy risk of electronic communications against the concomitant increase in personal ease, and often decide that convenience trumps privacy. But let the government propose to protect the public good by using data that Americans have freely provided to companies, and the citizenry become privacy dogmatists. No matter how many lives might be saved if the government could analyze nameless bytes of data for signs of deadly transactions, one's own alleged right not to have a government computer scan a database containing one's Christmas purchases is more important.

• *Never specify to what exactly in the proposed program you object.* Every element of TIA is now legal and already in effect. The government already has access to private databases for investigatory purposes, but searching them is extremely cumbersome for lack of decent software. Likewise, the government can legally search its own computers, but that capacity, too, is constrained by primitive technology. TIA's enemies have not called for

---

4. The Taliban was the ruling regime in Afghanistan before the United States ousted it for supporting al-Qaeda terrorists.

ending intelligence access to private or public databases, so their gripe ultimately boils down to the possibility that the government might do what it is already doing more efficiently. The rule appears to be of Luddite origin: The terrorists can expertly exploit our technology against us, but we must fight back with outdated, inadequate tools.

• *Confuse cause and effect.* TIA critics warn of impending totalitarianism should the research continue. A syndicated columnist for the *Orlando Sentinel* announced that the country was being "Stalinized." But totalitarian states do not arise because they marginally increase their access to personal data, they arise when social order is collapsing, as Amitai Etzioni has pointed out. The chance that the U.S. government will become a police state because it is better able to analyze private transactions for signs of terrorism is virtually nil; the chance would be greater, however, if the country were to experience a series of devastating attacks and confidence in the government's ability to protect the public safety were to evaporate.

An essential tool

The Pentagon's data mining project could easily go down in the next few months. A mongrel coalition of advocacy groups, ranging from the Free Congress Foundation and Grover Norquist's Americans for Tax Reform on the right to the ACLU [American Civil Liberties Union] on the left, has made the defeat of TIA its top priority for the year [2003]. [In 2002] a similar effort killed off TIPS—a Justice Department proposal for reporting possible terrorist activity. Senator Ron Wyden introduced an amendment [in January 2003] to defund TIA until Congress reviews it; other senators planning similar legislation include Dianne Feinstein, Daniel Inouye, and Russell Feingold. And the coalition of critics is pressuring a range of congressional committees to pull the plug. Should they succeed, Americans will be deprived of an essential tool to stop terrorist plots before they climax, even as al Qaeda's operatives are busily logging on and designing their next evil deed.

9

Facial Recognition Technology Can Enhance Homeland Security

Joseph Atick

In October 2001, when Joseph Atick issued the following remarks, he was chief executive officer of the Visionics Corporation, a leader in facial recognition technology. In 2002 Visionics merged with Identix, an industry leader in fingerprint identification technologies, and Atick now serves as Identix's president and CEO.

Facial recognition technology combines video cameras with special software in order to automatically scan crowds for wanted individuals. The video camera captures images of individuals' faces, which are automatically compared against a database of suspected terrorists. Relevant authorities are alerted if a match is found. Such a system does not permanently record the faces of those it scans, so the technology cannot be used to track the movement of ordinary citizens. Used at airports and other areas where security is a major concern, facial recognition technology has the potential to enhance security without resorting to inconvenient and invasive methods such as ID or fingerprint checks.

I'd like to start by iterating what I see is the cornerstone of our defense of the civilized world against crime and terrorism in this new era. I believe it's going to be our ability, in the context of a free society, to identify those who pose a threat to public safety and to prevent their actions.

Essential to the success of this defense strategy are intelligence data and identification technology, such as facial biometrics. The fact is terrorism and terrorists do not emerge overnight. They require indoctrination. They require constant reinforcement over an extended period of time. This affords intelligence agencies opportunities to establish their identities and to build watch lists. Ultimately terror is not faceless. . . .

[Terrorists] are at large, committing a crime, whether it's murder or [some] terrorist activity, and there's today no technology, apart from what

I'm talking about in terms of biometrics, that can stop these individuals from entering airports and facilities and conducting their activities.

According to published news reports, two of the terrorists of the September 11 [2001, terrorist attacks on America] were already on a watch list, sought by the FBI . . . but we had no facial recognition mechanism to stop them from entering the airport. A third was already known to the French authorities. I suspect when the dust settles, we'll find out that several others were already known to the Germans, Belgium, French, British, and Israeli intelligence organizations that have been collecting data about terror.

The technological challenge

While there is no guarantee that all terrorists will be known in advance, at the very least we have the responsibility to try to prevent the actions of the thousands already known, just like these. Given a watch list, . . . the question becomes: does the technology exist that can spot the individuals as they enter a country or attempt to board a plane?

The demands on such a technology are very high. It has to be able to do three things. One is scale, in that it should work across many security checkpoints at hundreds of airports and borders and not at just one location. It has to work as part of a network of cameras—it's not enough to just plug a hole in one door and leave every other door open. You have to be able to scale the application.

Second, just to give you the scale of the challenge technologically involved, you have to be able to sift through about six hundred million faces alone in the United States as they board planes, as they enter into security checkpoints each year, and spot the terrorists and criminals among them without interfering with the passenger flow. We do not want to create Draconian methods and barricades. The public will not accept that, nor will the airlines, nor will the airport authorities. We have to maintain throughput.

[Facial recognition technology] does not identify you or me. It is simply an alarm system that alerts when a terrorist on a watch list passes through.

Third, we have to function without infringing on the rights or inconveniencing the honest majority. We have to deliver a solution to a problem but without giving up something we have cherished so much, which is our privacy.

I believe there is good news here, which is that there is a technology. It is computerized facial recognition and facial scanning, such as the FaceIt® face recognition technology, which I can speak about because I'm not only the CEO of Visionics, the company that has commercially developed the technology, but I'm one of its main inventors. I've spent the last 14 years working on facial recognition and identification technologies, starting with my days in academia. I used to be the head of two laboratories where the human brain was studied to try to explore how we solve this problem.

The technology works as follows (it's very simple): you have a standard camera—it could be any video camera. It connects to what's called a FaceIt appliance, a small box where facial recognition runs. This technology captures each of the faces it sees in front of it, locates them in a crowd. It analyzes the face and creates a mathematical code, a digital code called a faceprint, which is essentially a description of the relationships between the landmarks of your face. It's some analytical measurement of the skull as it protrudes through the skin of your face. So it's some number, some mathematical relationship that's called a faceprint. It's only about 84 bytes of data, less than two sentences in an e-mail you send to a friend—that's what captures your identity.

Now this faceprint is encoded, encrypted, and can be sent by a network connection to a database where a watch list exists, a most-wanted database, for matching. The faceprint is a code that only a computer can interpret. It's encrypted; it cannot be used to reconstitute the image of a face. Given the faceprint, you cannot see what the face looks like. It's unique to a given face, and it does not change with age, lighting, or viewing conditions. It ignores facial hair and other superficial changes of the face. In a sense, it's a fingerprint in your face.

Let's look at it at a system level. These cameras can exist at the security checkpoints as people are walking through them. This is a controlled environment, so you can control the lighting as people walk through it. The camera automatically captures the face, and through the appliance, encodes it into a faceprint, and through the network sends it to a matcher that compares the faceprints against the watch list of the most wanted. It could be in Washington; it could be in the airport.

An alarm system, not a video recording system

If a match is successful and beyond a certain level of confidence, then it sends a message to an alarm system. The system is similar to burglar or fire alarms. They are monitored by a central agency, which says, "there's an alarm that happened, let me check." Video will not be shipped to that location. [Instead,] at the point when the alarm happens, an image of the person going through the security checkpoint and an image from the database appear on the screen in front of the person in the control monitoring the alarm. If the person believes that that is a true match, then they can signal back via a wireless connection to the airport or back via whatever mechanism is appropriate to the security guard at the gate and ask them to intercept and interview that passenger.

I want to emphasize if there is no match, then there is no memory—the image is dropped. This is not a recording system. It does not record any video, nor will you see any video from the other side. All that is shipped by the network is the 84 bytes of data. The system does not record, store, or alter the watch-list database in any way. The watch-list database cannot be hacked into, and because it only accepts faceprint queries; it doesn't take any delete or add or change.

Over the years, we have seen successive technologies adopted to enhance security. Today at security checkpoints like these, X-ray luggage scanners, metal detectors, chemical trace detectors are deployed to check for concealed weapons and explosives on our body or in our carry-on luggage. I see facial scanning and matching against the watch list as an integral component in tomorrow's airport security systems. I believe it's time to ensure that airports are no longer safe havens for criminals and terrorists. The American public agrees. In a recent Harris Poll conducted after September 11, 86 percent of the public endorsed the use of facial recognition to spot terrorists.

Facial scanning at airports is a tool, just like metal detectors and luggage scanners.

Still, there have been some criticisms of this technology. I would like to quickly address those. On the issue of privacy, it's important to emphasize that FaceIt surveillance system is not a national ID. It does not identify you or me. It is simply an alarm system that alerts when a terrorist on a watch list passes through a metal detector at the airport. If there is no match, I repeat, there is no memory.

Furthermore, such a system delivers security in a nondiscriminatory fashion. This is very important. FaceIt technology is based on analytical measurements that are independent of race, ethnic origination, or religion. It is free of human prejudices or profiling. It does not care where you come from and what your skin color looks like. We have gone further, actually, and have called for congressional oversight and federal legislation to ensure the watch lists contain only individuals who threaten public safety and to penalize for misuse of such technology down the line. I believe Congress will take action in due time, but at the moment their priorities are the real and present danger of terrorism and not on the theoretical potential of misuse down the line.

The technology will work

Another objection concerns the effectiveness of the technology. Actually the same people who raise the objection about privacy have pointed out and raised the same objection about the ineffectiveness of the technology. Some have used old data, for example, going back to a 1996 INS [Immigration and Naturalization Service] study. I'll give you the facts about that study. INS began in 1996 to try a mechanism to allow people to expedite their passage through the border. That was a very ambitious program early on in 1996. However, through reorganization of INS, the control of the border for vehicles was assigned to the Department of Transportation. As the Department of Transportation had no experts in biometrics, they suspended the project without any data being collected, without any results being analyzed. This is 1996; the world was so far different than we are today.

They also used data out of context, such as a Defense Department study, which, in fact, was a comparative analysis to check which algorithms are worthy of adoption for the embassy security project. In fact, DARPA [Defense Advanced Research Projects Agency] ended up recommending to Congress a $50 million four-year project called Human ID at a Distance, to adopt facial recognition for needs in embassies outside the United States.

So a lot of talk about using this type of data has been out of context and old and has said, without explaining it, that the technology does not work. I have two responses to that. First, technology is constantly evolving and advancing. Anybody who is in the science and technology business knows that the state of the art today is a quantum leap of where it was even a year ago, let alone five years ago. And of course, with the accelerated R&D initiatives under way around the world with university people as well as industrial people working together, the technology will rapidly become even more reliable and robust. It's a matter of time, whether it's this year, next year, the year after, it will be there.

FaceIt has already been used in many real-world environments and has produced significant results; the Mexican election system, police mug shot systems [in] many places around the world, criminal alarm systems in London, Birmingham, Iceland, International Airport Tampa, and so on.

But this is not my main point on this issue. My main point is this: facial scanning at airports is a tool, just like metal detectors and luggage scanners. They enhance security without having to be technologically perfect. A facial scanning system at the security checkpoint will alert the security guard to investigate, just like they do today when the metal detector beeps. Such a system will deter terrorists from boarding planes, just like metal detectors deter them from taking weapons on board, even though we all know metal detectors or luggage scanners are nowhere near a hundred percent accuracy. So if you say that facial recognition is not a hundred percent, well then, let's go ahead and take out all metal detectors and all luggage scanners, and let's see what happens to airport security.

We owe it to the traveling public to do everything in our capacity to ensure their safety. We have the technology today, as a nation, to peacefully and responsibly make a difference in the war against terror and to restore the public's trust in the travel process, without a cost, in my opinion, to the privacy of the honest majority. I see no legitimate objection why we should not do it.

10

Facial Recognition Technology Threatens Individual Privacy

David Kopel and Michael Krause

David Kopel is a research director and Michael Krause is a senior fellow at the Independence Institute.

Facial recognition technology (FRT), which has already been installed at some airports in the United States and was used by security personnel at Super Bowl XXXV in January 2001, has a dismal record of failure. Through a combination of video cameras and computer software, the technology is supposed to be able to identify individuals, such as terrorists or criminals, within a crowd. But in previous tests the technology has failed to recognize targeted individuals, falsely identified others, and been easily fooled by small changes in the targeted individual's appearance. However, the bigger problem with FRT is the threat it poses to individual privacy. If the technology ever starts to work, it could easily be used to construct a massive database that records individual's movements and actions without their knowledge.

W hen construction worker Rob Milliron sat down to eat his lunch in Tampa's [Florida] Ybor City entertainment district in July 2001, he didn't expect that it would result in a visit to his workplace by police officers looking to arrest him. His innocent dining inadvertently placed him in a showcase for one of the hottest trends in high-tech surveillance security: facial recognition cameras.

Milliron's face, scanned by the cameras, ended up in a *U.S. News & World Report* article about the technology. The accompanying headline read: "You can't hide those lying eyes in Tampa." Then a woman in Oklahoma saw the picture, misidentified Milliron as her ex-husband, who was wanted on child neglect charges, and called the police. After convincing police he had never been married, had kids, or even been to Oklahoma, he told the *St. Petersburg Times*, "They made me feel like a criminal."

Milliron perhaps can take some comfort from the fact that, as the use of facial recognition technology (FRT) for police work spreads, he won't be alone in being falsely suspected. FRT advocates offer Americans a sweet-sounding deal: sell your privacy for security. That's an especially comforting pitch in the wake of [the September 11, 2001, terrorist attacks on America]. We've all seen the grainy photos of [terrorist] Mohammed Atta and crew waltzing through airport security. If only those cameras had been linked to the proper criminal databases, say FRT proponents, the attackers never would have made it onto the planes.

"The biggest problem with face recognition systems is the simple fact that we don't know who terrorists are and law enforcement doesn't have their pictures."

But FRT, currently used in at least two U.S. cities and widespread throughout Great Britain, is notoriously unreliable and ineffective. At its best, it brings to our streets the high-tech equivalent of the Department of Transportation's airport security policy: humiliate and search everyone ineffectively.

That's bad enough, but the real problems will occur if FRT ever does start working as promised. It threatens to create a creepy future of ubiquitous spy cameras that will be used by police for purposes far less noble than thwarting terrorists.

FRT works by combining photographic images with computer databases. After an image is captured by a camera, a computer program measures some of the 80 or so nodal points on your face, such as the distance between your eyes, the width of your nose, the depth of your eye sockets, and the length of your jaw line. The technology then turns the nodal measurements into a numerical code called a "faceprint." A properly working face recognition system supposedly can match a person standing in front of a camera with a record from a database including tens of millions of faceprints. Criminals, say proponents, would have nowhere to hide. And law-abiding citizens would have no reason to fear.

A poor record of success

Yet for the most part, FRT hasn't worked as intended. The Milliron incident in Tampa was just one of a string of national flops for face scanners, which prior to 9/11 were widely derided even as they were being implemented or considered by several municipalities, including Tampa; Jacksonville, Florida; and Virginia Beach, Virginia. At the time, FRT was being marketed as a tool to catch wanted felons and find runaways and missing persons. Nonetheless, a measure was introduced in the Virginia legislature requiring a judge's approval to use FRT, and in Tampa city council members who had approved its use claimed they had been fooled and didn't know what they had voted for.

Then the terrorists attacked, and everything seemed to change. The Virginia legislature dropped the bill requiring judicial approval. Executives at FRT firms testified before Congress and were called on by intelligence and law enforcement agencies. Tom Colatosti, CEO of Viisage Technology, told reporters, "If our technology had been deployed, the likelihood is [the terrorists] would have been recognized." Major airports, including Boston's Logan, Dallas-Fort Worth International, and Palm Beach International, have installed test versions of FRT. While the stock market was slumping, scanning companies Visionics and Identix saw their share prices shoot up 244 percent and 197 percent, respectively, in the six months following 9/11. (The two companies have since merged and are now known as Identix.)

Yet one stubborn fact remains: FRT doesn't work. In March [2002], Palm Beach International Airport ran a test of Visionics' "Argus" facial recognition system (a version that can be plugged into existing closed circuit TV systems) at its Concourse C security checkpoint. Fifteen airport employees tried to get through the security checkpoint. The security checkers had a database of 250 faceprints, including those of the 15 testers. Over a four-week period, the testers made 958 attempts to pass through the checkpoint; the face recognition system stopped them 455 times, for a success rate of only 47 percent. On top of that, there were 1,081 false alarms triggered by ordinary passengers and other airport employees passing through the scanners. That worked out to two or three false alarms per hour.

In the experiment, the people who triggered false positives didn't have to be pulled aside and interrogated by the police. But imagine what would happen if they did; imagine FRT on every concourse of the airport, using a database of "wanted" suspects numbering in the hundreds of thousands. That would make for at least dozens of false positives every hour.

What happens if you're one of the folks detained? After the police have marched you into the interrogation room, how do you prove that you're really who your identification says you are, and not a terrorist (or an ordinary fugitive) using false ID? If you're one of the airport cops, how do you go about your job knowing that the overwhelming majority of the suspects are in fact innocent?

The Palm Beach test isn't the only one that casts a shadow on FRT. Richard Smith, former head of the Privacy Foundation at Denver University and now a privacy and Internet security consultant in Brookline, Massachusetts, conducted his own test of the Visionics "FaceIt" system. He got similarly unimpressive results.

Smith found that changes in lighting, eyeglasses, background objects, camera position, and facial position and expression all seriously affected image quality and system efficacy. He concluded that airport use of FRT would require "special walkways where lighting is tightly controlled and passengers pass single file." Passengers would have to be "instructed to remove hats and glasses and look straight ahead at a head-height camera."

Seriously flawed technology

None of this fits with the exaggerated claims in favor of FRT made by those selling it and repeated as fact by gullible media outlets. According to the *Denver Post*, "It doesn't matter if you gain 200 pounds or go bald between photographs. Short of plastic surgery the camera will recognize you." Unless, of course, you put on sunglasses, or cock your head, or make a funny face.

Or get older. A study by the National Institute of Standards and Technology found a 43 percent failure rate for pictures of the same person taken one and a half years apart. Similarly, the Defense Department funded a test of commercially available FRT. It found that the systems failed one-third of the time and produced a large number of false positives. The impressive reliability rates you hear from the face scanning companies are usually based on tests in laboratories under optimal conditions.

Yet "even if the technology worked perfectly," Smith observes, "it would still allow 99 percent of the terrorists through . . . The biggest problem with face recognition systems is the simple fact that we don't know who the terrorists are and law enforcement doesn't have their pictures. Spotting terrorists at airports is simply the wrong use of this technology."

Even if we did know who the terrorists were, we'd have to sit them all down for a session with [photographer] Annie Leibovitz for FRT to be useful. According to the testers at Palm Beach International, "Input photographs needed to be of good quality to make successful matches." Similarly, people being scanned need to stand still, look straight at the camera, and not wear glasses. As the Palm Beach study acknowledged: "Motion of test subject head has a significant effect on system ability. There was substantial loss in matching if test subject had a pose 15 to 30 degrees off of input camera focal point and eyeglasses were problematic."

Even if we acknowledge that electronic government eyes are no different than a cop on every corner, do we really want that?

Mass face scanning was formally introduced to the American public in January 2001 at Super Bowl xxxv in Tampa, when football fans had their faces surreptitiously checked with a Viisage system and compared to a database of known criminals. The Tampa authorities then began to use scanning in the Ybor City entertainment district. They targeted people strolling down the street or eating lunch, comparing their faceprints to a database of criminals and runaways.

Using open record requests, the American Civil Liberties Union (ACLU) discovered that the system was essentially abandoned within months of its highly publicized rollout. No correct matches had been made to the criminal database. Instead, according to the ACLU, the system matched "male and female subjects and subjects with significant differences in age and weight."

Put another way, FRT can be dumber than [bumbling movie] Inspector Clouseau: Even he could distinguish a man from a woman, or a short fat man from a tall thin man. The Tampa police, for their part, deny they have abandoned FRT, saying they are revamping it to work with more cameras.

Before they spend the money, they should take a closer look at the experience in the world capital of FRT. The London borough of Newham, with a population of about 250,000, is widely touted by advocates as proof of the technology's awesome crime-fighting ability. Newham boasts approximately 300 government cameras located in strategic places and linked to Visionics' FaceIt system. Newham's FRT is credited by advocates and local government officials with cutting crime by nearly 40 percent since 1998. That effect, if real, was apparently not long-lasting. According to a United Press International report, street robberies and car theft—two crimes for which FRT is supposed to be an especially powerful deterrent—were on the rise again in Newham [in 2001].

And as Jeffrey Rosen reported in *The New York Times Magazine* last October [2001], the Newham spy system has not resulted in a single arrest during its three years of operation. Nor do the people who run the system even know who is in the database. The deterrent effect, to the extent there may be one, appears to lie with the signs posted throughout Newham telling criminals that cameras are watching and that the police know who they are, where they live, and what crimes they have committed. Of course, "it's not true," as the Newham monitoring chief admitted to Rosen.

Newham is simply a part of Great Britain's growing spy camera network, which arose as a response to terrorist bombings in London's financial district in the early 1990s. Britain now has some 1.5 million government cameras in place. As the cameras were first being set up, the government, then under the control of the Tories, insisted that "if you have nothing to hide, you have nothing to fear." Now under control of the Labour Party, the government is spending $115 million for still more spy cameras.

Despite ubiquitous cameras, however, violent and property crime in England is soaring. A three-year government study by the Scottish Center for Criminology recently concluded there is no evidence to suggest that Britain's spy cameras have reduced serious crime overall. Another study, this one by the National Association for the Care and Resettlement of Offenders, looked at 14 British cities and found that the cameras had little effect in reducing crime. The study suggested that improving street lighting would be a more cost-effective crime prevention method.

This much can be said in favor of the cameras: In some cases, they have been used to convict speeders, other traffic law offenders, and litterbugs. Yet it's one thing to give up your privacy to catch Irish Republican Army terrorists. It's another thing to surrender privacy so the police can catch people who litter.

The threat of facial image databases

Of course, just because FRT doesn't work very well today doesn't mean it will never work. FRT companies are receiving massive amounts of corporate welfare. According to a March General Accounting Office (GAO) report, as of June 2001 the Departments of Justice and Defense had given about $21.3 million and $24.7 million, respectively, to the research and development of FRT. All this research will probably result in much-improved products eventually.

What then? Philip Agre, an associate professor in the Information Studies Department of the University of California at Los Angeles, argues that as FRT gets better the potential for abuse will rise commensurately. "As the underlying information and communications technologies (digital cameras, image databases, processing power and data communications) become radically cheaper (and more powerful)," he writes on his Web site, "new facial image databases will not be hard to construct, with or without the consent of the people whose faces are captured."

Once those databases exist, their uses will doubtless expand, consistent with typical bureaucratic mission creep. Look, for example, at the 2001 Colorado law allowing the Division of Motor Vehicles (DMV) to use biometric technology to map applicants' faces for driver's licenses. The stated intent was to stop the same person from obtaining multiple licenses. But the law's language was much broader, allowing access to the DMV database to "aid a federal, state or local government agency in carrying out such agency's official function"—in other words, for any government purpose whatsoever. Illinois and West Virginia also have turned their driver's license bureaus into mandatory faceprint collection points.

In March [2002], after national criticism, the Colorado legislature refined the face mapping scheme, declaring that before a government agency can tap into the image database, it must have "a reasonable suspicion that a crime has been committed or will be committed and a reasonable suspicion that the image requested is either the perpetrator of such a crime or the victim of such a crime." Like Colorado, states can establish guidelines that ostensibly limit government use of your faceprint. But once your faceprint is in a state database, the federal government has legal authority to use it for any purpose at all. By federal statute, every state driver's license record is available to every federal agency, "including any court or law enforcement agency, in carrying out its functions." Because of the Supremacy Clause of the U.S. Constitution, a state government cannot limit the uses to which federal agencies put these state-gathered faceprints.

Face scanning is typically introduced and then expanded . . . without specific legislative permission.

Even before 9/11, many local law enforcement agencies considered political surveillance to be one of their official functions. For example, last spring [2002] it came to light that the Denver Police Intelligence Unit has for years kept surveillance files on government protesters, including about 3,000 individuals and 200 organizations. Among those targeted for police spying were the American Friends Service Committee (a Quaker group), Amnesty International, and Copwatch (a group that protests police brutality). The surveillance program was supposedly scaled back (though not eliminated), but only after secret documents were brought to public attention by the Colorado Civil Liberties Union.

Telling Colorado cops that they must have "reasonable suspicion" before accessing the faceprint database sounds good, but law enforcement will easily find ways around such restrictions. The Denver police surveillance guidelines have always required criminal suspicion, so the police simply listed as extremists the groups they wanted to spy on.

Indeed, the main constraint on the Denver Police Department's political spying program was manpower. There are only so many people a police unit can spy on at once. But with FRT, political surveillance may one day escape such limits. Consider a mobile monitoring unit equipped with a face scanning camera, face recognition software, and the state's driver's license faceprint database. It would be a simple matter to compile a list of everyone who attends a rally to protest police brutality, to denounce drug laws, or to oppose U.S. foreign policy.

Nor will the technology necessarily be confined to use at political protests. In July 2001, the conservative U.S. House Majority Leader Dick Armey (R-Texas) joined with the ACLU [American Civil Liberties Union] to warn: "Used in conjunction with facial recognition software . . . the Colorado database could allow the public movements of every citizen in the state to be identified, tracked, recorded and stored."

Sound far-fetched? On September 20, 2001, Joseph Atick, CEO of Visionics, told a Department of Transportation airport security committee that FaceIt, in conjunction with security cameras, could be linked via the Internet to a federal monitoring station and alert officials to a match within seconds. He added that virtually any camera, anywhere, could be linked to the system, as could a "wide network of databases."

Destroying individual privacy

Opponents of FRT should not count on much help from the courts. Standard legal doctrine holds that there is little or no expectation of privacy in public. There is nothing unconstitutional, for example, about a police officer's sitting on a bench at a shopping mall and making notes about the people who pass by. FRT advocates can argue that massive surveillance is simply like having 10—or 100—police officers in the mall, and that the quantitative difference is of no constitutional significance.

Yet even if we acknowledge that electronic government eyes are no different than a cop on every corner, do we really want that? One of the conclusions of Jeffrey Rosen's *New York Times Magazine* piece on spy cameras in Great Britain was that the cameras are designed not to produce arrests but to make people feel they are being watched all the time. "The people behind [the cameras] are zooming in on unconventional behavior in public that has nothing to do with terrorism," Rosen wrote. "And rather than thwarting serious crime, the cameras are being used to enforce social conformity in ways that Americans may prefer to avoid."

There is some reason for hope, however. In the past, U.S. courts have acknowledged that technological change can make a constitutional difference. Under 19th-century constitutional doctrine, there was no need for the police to get a warrant before eavesdropping. If a policeman stood on public property and could hear a conversation going on inside a house, he did not need a search warrant. That doctrine made sense in the 1800s; if you talk so loudly that people on the sidewalk can hear you, you don't have a legitimate expectation of privacy for your words.

But in the 1967 case *Katz v. United States*, the Supreme Court considered the issue raised by police officers who, without trespassing on private property, used parabolic microphones or wiretaps to listen in on conversations. Justice Hugo Black said this kind of surveillance was permissible because the new technology was simply an updated version of eavesdropping. The majority of the Court, however, ruled that wiretaps and other electronic surveillance should be permitted only if the police obtained a search warrant. The intrusiveness of electronic surveillance, its great potential for abuse, and its infringement on traditional expectations of privacy all distinguished it from old-fashioned eavesdropping.

Similarly, widespread face scanning could eventually make it possible for the government to track the movement of most citizens most of the time. It would expand the government's tracking capability by several orders of magnitude—as great an increase as the one from human ears to parabolic microphones.

Like the Fourth Amendment itself, *Katz* relies on a subjective judgment of reasonableness. Thus, there is no guarantee that *Katz* would stand as a barrier to omnipresent British-style face scanning; nor would *Katz* necessarily forbid placing information about every person's movements in a permanent government database.

Ultimately, the future of face scanning will depend on the political process. There is almost no chance that the American public or their elected officials would vote in favor of tracking everyone all the time. Yet face scanning is typically introduced and then expanded by administrative fiat, without specific legislative permission.

So there is a strong possibility that future Americans will be surprised to learn from history books that in the first centuries of American independence citizens took for granted that the government did not and could not monitor all of their movements and activities in public places.

11

Ethnic Profiling to Prevent Terrorism Is Justified

Michael Kinsley

Michael Kinsley is the editor of the online magazine Slate *and a weekly columnist for the* Washington Post.

Singling out Arab-looking individuals at airports to prevent terrorist acts or for other homeland security purposes is discriminatory, but nevertheless justifiable. In considering the legality of ethnic profiling, it is necessary to weigh practical considerations of harms and benefits. Inconveniencing Arab men through airport ID checks is justified because the small harm done, in the form of inconvenience and embarrassment, is outweighed by the benefit to public safety.

When thugs menace someone because he looks Arabic, that's racism. When airport security officials single out Arabic-looking men for a more intrusive inspection, that's something else. What is the difference? The difference is that the airport security folks have a rational reason for what they do. An Arab-looking man heading toward a plane is statistically more likely to be a terrorist. That likelihood is infinitesimal, but the whole airport rigmarole is based on infinitesimal chances. If trying to catch terrorists this way makes sense at all, then . . . logic says you should pay more attention to people who look like Arabs than to people who don't. This is true even if you are free of all ethnic prejudices. It's not racism.

But that doesn't make it OK. Much of the discrimination that is outlawed in this country—correctly outlawed, we (almost) all agree—could be justified, often sincerely, by reasons other than racial prejudice. Without the civil rights laws, employers with nothing personal against blacks might well decide that hiring whites is more cost-efficient than judging each jobseeker on his or her individual merits. Universities could base their admissions policies on the valid assumption that whites, on average, are better-prepared for college. Even though this white advantage is the result of past and present racism, these decisions themselves might be rational and not racially motivated.

All decisions about whom to hire, whom to admit, whose suitcase to ransack as he's rushing to catch a plane are based on generalizations from observable characteristics to unobservable ones. But even statistically valid generalizations are wrong in particular instances. (Many blacks are better prepared for college than many whites. Virtually every Arab hassled at an airport is not a terrorist.) Because even rational discrimination has victims, and because certain generalizations are especially poisonous, America has decided that these generalizations (about race, gender, religion, and so on) are morally wrong. They are wrong even if they are statistically valid, and even if not acting on them imposes a real cost.

We're at war with a terror network that just killed 6,000 innocents. . . . Are we really supposed to ignore the one identifiable fact we know about them?

Until recently, the term "racial profiling" referred to the police practice of pulling over black male drivers disproportionately, on the statistically valid but morally offensive assumption that black male drivers are more likely to be involved in crime. Now the term has become virtually a synonym for racial discrimination. But if "racial profiling" means anything specific at all, it means rational discrimination: racial discrimination with a non-racist rationale. The question is: When is that OK?

The tempting answer is never: Racial discrimination is wrong no matter what the rationale. Period. But today we're at war with a terror network that just killed 6,000 innocents [during the September 11, 2001, terrorist attacks on America] and has anonymous agents in our country planning more slaughter.[1] Are we really supposed to ignore the one identifiable fact we know about them? That may be asking too much.

Justifiable discrimination

And there is another complication in the purist view: affirmative action. You can believe (as I do) that affirmative action is often a justifiable form of discrimination, but you cannot sensibly believe that it isn't discrimination at all. Racial profiling and affirmative action are analytically the same thing. When the cops stop black drivers or companies make extra efforts to hire black employees, they are both giving certain individuals special treatment based on racial generalizations. The only difference is that in one case the special treatment is something bad and in the other it's something good. Yet defenders of affirmative action tend to deplore racial profiling and vice versa.

The truth is that racial profiling and affirmative action are both dangerous medicines that are sometimes appropriate. So when is "sometimes"? It seems obvious to me, though not to many others, that discrimination in favor of historically oppressed groups is less offensive than

---

1. Official estimates now put the number of people killed in the September 11 attacks at just over three thousand.

discrimination against them. Other than that, the considerations are practical. How much is at stake in forbidding a particular act of discrimination? How much is at stake in allowing it?

A generalization from stereotypes may be statistically rational, but is it necessary? When you're storming a plane looking for the person who has planted a bomb somewhere, there isn't time to avoid valid generalizations and treat each person as an individual. At less urgent moments, like airport check-in, the need to use ethnic identity as a shortcut is less obvious. And then there are those passengers in Minneapolis [in September 2001] who insisted that three Arab men (who had cleared security) be removed from the plane. These people were making a cost, benefit, and probability analysis so skewed that it amounts to simple racism. (And Northwest Airlines' acquiescence was shameful.)

So what about singling out Arabs at airport security checkpoints? I am skeptical of the value of these check-in rituals in general, which leads me to suspect that the imposition on a minority is not worth it. But assuming these procedures do work, it's hard to argue that helping to avoid another September 11 is not worth the imposition, which is pretty small: inconvenience and embarrassment, as opposed to losing a job or getting lynched.

A colleague says that people singled out at airport security should be consoled with frequent flier miles. They're already getting an even better consolation: the huge increase in public sensitivity to anti-Muslim and anti-Arab prejudice, which President [George W.] Bush—to his enormous credit—has made such a focal point of his response to September 11. And many victims of racial profiling at the airport may not need any consolation. After all, they don't want to be hijacked and blown up either.

12

Ethnic Profiling Is Unfair and Ineffective

David Cole and James X. Dempsey

David Cole is the Nation's *legal affairs correspondent. James X. Dempsey is deputy director of the Center for Democracy and Technology, an organization that promotes democratic values and constitutional liberties in the digital age. Cole and Dempsey are co-authors of* Terrorism & the Constitution: Sacrificing Civil Liberties in the Name of National Security, *from which the following viewpoint is excerpted.*

Ethnic profiling is neither a legal nor an effective response to terrorism. It is illegal because the equal protection clause of the Constitution prohibits government authorities from relying on racial or ethnic distinctions in detaining individuals. It is ineffective because it alienates the minority and immigrant communities who could be helping law enforcement identify true terrorist threats. The use of ethnicity is justified in limited circumstances, such as in the immediate aftermath of a crime when ethnicity is used as an identifying trait. But when law enforcement authorities use ethnicity as a predictor of future behavior, as is the case with ethnic profiling, they are engaging in unjustified discrimination and poor security procedures.

One of the most dramatic responses to the [terrorist] attack of September 11 [2001] was a swift reversal in public attitudes about racial and ethnic profiling as a law enforcement tool. Before September 11, about 80 percent of the American public considered racial profiling wrong. State legislatures, local police departments, and the President had all ordered data collection on the racial patterns of stops and searches. The U.S. Customs Service, sued for racial profiling, had instituted measures to counter racial and ethnic profiling at the borders. And a federal law on racial profiling seemed likely.

After September 11, however, polls reported that 60 percent of the American public favored ethnic profiling, at least as long as it was directed at Arabs and Muslims. The fact that the perpetrators of the September 11 attack were all Arab men, and that the attack appears to have been orchestrated by al Qaeda, led many to believe that it is only common sense to pay closer attention to Arab-looking men boarding airplanes and elsewhere. And the high stakes—there is reason to believe that we will be subjected to further terrorist attacks—make the case for engaging in profiling stronger here than in routine drug interdiction stops on highways. Thus, Stuart Taylor, a columnist for *Newsweek*, the *National Journal*, and *Legal Times*, wrote shortly after the attacks in favor of ethnic profiling of Arab men on airplanes.

The use of ethnic stereotypes is certainly not "necessary" to effective law enforcement.

Press accounts made clear that whether as a matter of official policy or not, law enforcement officials were paying closer attention to those who appear to be Arabs and Muslims. And . . . the Justice Department announced its intention to interview 5,000 young immigrant men, based solely on their age, immigrant status, and the country from which they came. Virtually all of those interviewed were Arabs and Muslims, and the list looked uncomfortably like one generated to identify Arab and Muslims without explicitly relying on ethnicity. Several police departments around the country refused to participate in the interviews on the grounds that they appeared to constitute ethnic profiling.

There is no question that the immediate aftermath of September 11 called for greater urgency than the ongoing war on drugs, and that the immediate threat posed to our national security was greater. But that does not answer whether ethnic profiling is a legal, much less an effective, response. The argument that we cannot afford to rely on something other than racial or ethnic proxies for suspicion, after all, is precisely the rationale used to intern 110,000 persons of Japanese ancestry during World War II. While subjecting an individual to closer inspection and a possible search is less extreme than detention, the rationale—that we should rely on ethnic background as a proxy for suspicion—is the same.

Ethnic profiling and the Constitution

Precisely because of the history of racial discrimination in this country, the Equal Protection Clause of the Constitution presumptively forbids government authorities from relying on explicit racial or ethnic distinctions. Such actions trigger "strict scrutiny," a stringent form of court review that requires the government to justify its racial distinctions by showing that they are "narrowly tailored," or "necessary," to further a "compelling government interest." There is no question that protecting citizens from terrorism is a compelling government interest, but so too is drug interdiction—in fact, all criminal law enforcement would likely be viewed as a compelling state interest.

The real question from a constitutional perspective is whether the means adopted—reliance on ethnic appearance as a proxy for suspicion—is narrowly tailored to further that interest. It is highly unlikely that profiling could satisfy that scrutiny. First, the vast majority of persons who appear Arab and Muslim—probably well over 99.9 percent—have no involvement with terrorism. Arab and Muslim appearance, in other words, is a terribly inaccurate proxy for terrorism. In the sex discrimination context, where the Supreme Court applies less stringent scrutiny than it does to ethnic or racial discrimination, the court held that statistics showing that 2 percent of young men between the ages of 18 and 21 had been arrested for drunk driving did not justify denying men of that age the right to purchase an alcoholic beverage.

Second, the use of ethnic stereotypes is certainly not "necessary" to effective law enforcement. In fact, it is likely to be bad law enforcement. When one treats a whole group of people as presumptively suspicious, it means that agents are more likely to miss dangerous persons who take care not to fit the profile. In addition, the fact that the vast majority of those suspected on the basis of their Arab or Muslim appearance are innocent will inevitably cause agents to let their guard down. Overbroad generalizations, in other words, are problematic not only because they constitute an unjustified imposition on innocents, but because they undermine effective law enforcement.

What is particularly troubling about the government's response to September 11 is that government officials seemed determined to apply ethnic profiling on a nationwide, seemingly arbitrary basis.

Profiling undermines effective law enforcement in still another way. It is virtually certain to alienate members of the targeted communities. Studies of policing have shown that it is far more effective to work with communities than against them. Where a community trusts law enforcement, people are more likely to obey the law, and more likely to cooperate with the police in identifying and bringing to justice wrongdoers in their midst. If we have reason to believe that there are potential terrorist threats within the Arab and Muslim community in the United States, we should be seeking ways to work with the millions of law-abiding members of those communities to help identify the true threats, not treating the entire community as suspect.

Narrow, compelling interests vs. broad generalizations

The ethnic profiling issue is complicated in the wake of the September 11 attacks by the fact that some use of ethnicity is probably permissible. When a bank reports a robbery, and describes the robbers as three white men in their thirties wearing blue shirts, the police can rely on race in seeking to identify and catch the suspects. In that setting, the use of race does not carry negative stereotyped connotations, but is simply an identifying marker, like the fact that they were wearing blue shirts. Moreover, as one of the few identifying characteristics, reliance on race in that setting is narrowly tailored to the compelling interest of catching the robbers. Ethnic or racial profiling, by contrast, consists of the reliance on race as a generalization about future behavior—the assumption that because an individual is black, he is more likely to rob a bank. Such reliance on generalizations is probably always impermissible, whereas reliance on race as an identifying criterion is usually permissible.

In the aftermath of September 11, it was often difficult to separate out these two uses of ethnicity. If law enforcement agents had reason to believe that there were others involved in the planning and carrying out of the attacks or that their associates might have been planning further attacks, and that these others were Arab or Muslim men, then relying on ethnic criteria to identify the guilty parties may have been permissible.

However, to the extent that law enforcement agents rely on ethnicity as a predictor of future behavior, they are using impermissible generalizations. Where the perpetrators are thought to be planning future attacks, the distinction between an identifying criterion and a prospective generalization is particularly difficult to draw. Therefore, where ethnicity is being accorded a dominant role in investigative activities, two other factors become very important. First, the use of an ethnic identifying factor becomes more objectionable when it is applied on a nationwide basis over an extended period of time. It is one thing to say that the police, having only the information that three white men robbed a bank, can stop and question all white men in the vicinity of the bank immediately after the robbery. It would be another matter for the police nationwide to keep interviewing white males until they find the bank robbers.

Second, when the government relies on ethnic identifying characteristics, it is critical that it act quickly to resolve its suspicions and to determine whether other, non-ethnic factors justify or disprove its selection of certain people for scrutiny. What is particularly troubling about the government's response to September 11 is that government officials seemed determined to apply ethnic profiling on a nationwide, seemingly arbitrary basis and failed to resolve promptly their selection of certain individuals for the worst form of ethnic-based action: detention without serious criminal charges.

13

Immigration Must Be Restricted to Protect America Against Terrorists

Mark Krikorian

Mark Krikorian is executive director of the Center for Immigration Studies, a think tank based in Washington, D.C.

Immigration and border controls are a vital aspect of homeland security. However, the huge levels of immigration throughout the 1990s and since 2000 have overwhelmed the agencies charged with ensuring that suspected terrorists do not enter the United States. In addition, terrorists take advantage of large immigrant populations in the United States, hiding in immigrant communities and even recruiting other terrorists from these communities. For these reasons, restricting Arab or Muslim immigration to the United States would help prevent terrorists from entering the United States—but such a policy would also be discriminatory. Therefore, in the interest of homeland security, the sheer volume of overall immigration must be reduced.

In the year since [the September 11, 2001, terrorist attacks on America], there has developed a new consensus on the need for tighter immigration enforcement and border controls. Gone are the days when *The Wall Street Journal* repeatedly called for a constitutional amendment that would say "There shall be open borders." Since September 11, even the Libertarian-Left united front for open borders, which so successfully obstructed immigration enforcement in the past, has at least had to pay lip service to the importance of border control.

This change has manifested itself in many ways. The USA Patriot Act, [2001's] major piece of anti-terrorism legislation, contained immigration-related provisions that, among other things, finally gave the INS [Immigration and Naturalization Service] and State Department access to the FBI's criminal databases. The border security bill signed by the president [George W. Bush] in May [2002] includes a mandate for the creation of a

Mark Krikorian, "Safety in (Lower) Numbers: Immigration and Homeland Security," *Center for Immigration Studies Backgrounder*, October 2002, pp. 1–7. Copyright © 2002 by Center for Immigration Studies. Reproduced by permission.

visa containing a fingerprint or other identifier to be used by "nonimmigrant" foreigners (tourists, students, businessmen, etc.)—so that the INS would actually know whether a visitor leaves when his time expires, something we cannot now determine.

The agencies responsible for immigration have also made changes. The INS, for instance, decided that it should start looking for the 300,000-plus foreigners who have absconded after being ordered deported, and these names are being entered into the FBI's national crime database (though only about 900 have so far been located). And the State Department now requires more intensive examination of visa applications by young men from Muslim countries.

There is much left to accomplish in the area of border control—for instance, the INS still has a laughably small number of investigators, while the State Department's manual for visa officers still says that "Advocating terrorism, through oral or written statements is usually not a sufficient ground for finding an applicant ineligible." Though such details matter greatly, the principle of sovereign borders is no longer a matter of mainstream debate.

The INS has collected in underground limestone vaults some 2 million documents filed by immigrants but lost or forgotten by the agency.

But what about the actual level of immigration?

The idea of any connection between immigration and terrorism has been dismissed by many policymakers and activists. INS Commissioner James Ziglar, for instance, piously observed that "We're not talking about immigration, we're talking about evil." Elsewhere he even employed the "then the terrorists will win" cliche, saying, "If, in response to the events of September 11, we engage in excess and shut out what has made America great, then we will have given the terrorists a far greater victory than they could have hoped to achieve."

Groups lobbying in favor of mass immigration rushed to make the same point after the attacks. Cecilia Munoz of the National Council of La Raza gamely averred that "There's no relationship between immigration and terrorism." And Jeanne Butterfield, executive director of the American Immigration Lawyers Association (and former head of the Marxist Palestine Solidarity Committee), echoed this denial of reality: "I don't think the events [on September 11] attributed to the failure of our immigration laws."

And indeed to argue that cuts in the level ofimmigration are necessary for homeland security might appear a bit opportunistic, like apologists for farm subsidies talking about "food security." After all, it's only Muslim fanatics who are trying to murder our children, not Mexican dishwashers or Filipino nurses.

But there are two compelling reasons why a reduction in the legal admission of foreign citizens across the board—both permanent immigrants as well as temporary visa-holders, such as students, workers, and exchange visitors—is imperative for homeland security. One reason is short-term and practical, the second long-term and strategic.

An overloaded agency

The practical reason is that the INS simply cannot function as it should at the current level of admissions. It is sobering to review the list of responsibilities heaped on the INS over the past year [2002]:

- Develop an automated entry-exit visa tracking system for 500 million annual border crossings;
- Develop a foreign-student tracking system;
- Enforce the requirement that non-citizens report any change of address within 10 days;
- Fingerprint, photograph, and track all visitors from Iran, Iraq, Sudan, and Libya, plus men ages 16 to 45 from Saudi Arabia, Pakistan and Yemen, plus selected Egyptians and Jordanians (and the list is likely to grow);
- Completely overhaul its internal organizational structure and/or shift all or part of the agency to the newly formed Department of Homeland Security;
- Hire and train thousands of new employees;
- Implement a 30-point "smart border" plan with Canada;
- Review tens of thousands of asylum cases to identify any immigrants who have acknowledged being accused of links to terrorism abroad;
- Report to Congress every two years (instead of every five) on each Visa Waiver country's participation in that program;
- Report to Congress each year the number of deportation absconders; and
- Fully integrate all internal databases and make them interoperable with a new system that will allow sharing of information with law enforcement and intelligence agencies. The new system "shall be searchable based on linguistically sensitive algorithms that (i) account for variations in name formats and transliterations, including varied spellings and varied separation or combination of name elements, within a particular language; and (ii) incorporate advanced linguistic, mathematical, statistical, and anthropological research and methods."

All this in addition to its enormous pre-9/11 workload.

Now, one might argue that more money would help the INS reform itself and tackle security issues without cutting immigration. This is exactly what Congress and the administration have in mind—the agency's FY 2002 budget was up 15 percent from the prior year, and the proposed 2003 budget would grow another 12 percent to $6.3 billion.

This additional funding would be desperately needed even without concerns over homeland security. The General Accounting Office reported in May 2001 that the receipt of new applications (for green cards, citizenship, temporary workers, etc.) increased 50 percent over six years and the backlog of unresolved applications quadrupled to nearly four million. The number of citizenship applications filed in the 1990s was about 6.9 million, triple the level of the 1980s; temporary admissions nearly doubled in the 1990s to more than 30 million: and the number of (very labor-intensive) applications for asylum in the 1990s was nearly one million, more than double the level of the 1980s.

Choking on paperwork. This tidal wave of immigration has over-whelmed the INS bureaucracy. The redoubtable Marcus Stern of the Copley News Service first reported this summer [2002] that the INS has collected in underground limestone vaults some 2 million documents filed by immigrants but lost or forgotten by the agency. In the words of one INS spokesman, "The field offices weren't sure what to do with all of the documents they had not been able to look through, and they were a bit overwhelmed by the unprecedented growth" in immigration.

Among these two million orphaned documents are 200,000 unfiled change-of-address cards, contributing to the government's inability to find half of the 5,000 non-citizens whom Justice Department officials wanted to interview in the wake of the terrorist attacks. This disarray is being exacerbated by Attorney General John Ashcroft's . . . announcement that the INS would resume enforcement of a long-ignored law requiring legal immigrants to submit change-of-address notification within 10 days of moving. As a result, the INS has received hundreds of thousands of such forms, a tenfold increase over the previous year. In the words of an INS spokesman, "They've literally swamped our ability to keep up with the flow." What's more, the INS does not process these address changes through a database, but rather places each one, by hand, in the individual's paper file. . . .

Immigrant communities act as the sea in which . . . terrorists can swim like fish.

Reorganize for success? To address the agency's many problems, there have been various plans to reorganize the INS by separating its service and enforcement functions, with rival Administration and congressional proposals. The administration's plan for the new Department of Homeland Security would move the entire INS into the new agency.[1] . . .

But however the INS is reorganized, and how ever much money is allocated to it, such measures can never be adequate. The only way to give the INS the breathing room it needs to put its house in order and to address homeland security concerns is to reduce its workload wherever possible. Some demands upon the agency can't be reduced—even with tighter visa controls, most tourists will continue to come, and legal immigrants will continue applying for citizenship (and, in fact, citizenship applications through July 2002 were up 58 percent from the same period in the prior year).

Cut the numbers. But the admission of new immigrants and foreign students and workers is an area where the INS's load can be lightened dramatically. The visa lottery, for instance, ought to be eliminated. It provides 50,000 visas each year based on little but random chance to people from countries not among the top 14 immigrant-sending nations (the visa lottery admits a disproportionate number of Middle Easterners).

Likewise, the immigration of relatives should be limited to the spouses and minor children of American citizens, bringing an end to spe-

---

1. In February 2003 the INS was officially subsumed into the Department of Homeland Security.

cial immigration rights for adult sons and daughters, parents, and siblings who have their own families. In addition, employment-based immigration should be limited to those with exceptional abilities which cannot be replicated in the United States—portions of what are now called the First and Second Employment-based Preferences. This would have the added benefit of mostly eliminating the extremely time-consuming process of labor certifications.

Adding to these categories a modest number of authentic refugees, genuinely in need of immediate resettlement, would bring the annual number of green cards issued down from over one million last year to around 300,000. And placing caps on the bewildering array of student and worker visas (and eliminate some categories) would stop, or even reverse, the very rapid growth in these programs. Only in this way can the INS get the essential breathing room needed if it is ever to be able to fulfill its role in homeland defense.

Terrorist fish in the sea

But once the INS takes advantage of a respite in mass immigration to craft a functioning border-control system, then what? Are there long-term security reasons for *keeping* immigration relatively low?

Whatever one thinks of the debates over immigration's other impacts, the security implications of large foreign-born populations in a world of easy and cheap transportation and communications cannot be wished away. In such a world, immigrant communities act as the sea within which, as Mao might have said, terrorists can swim like fish.

President Bush used a different image in his address to the joint session of Congress after the 9/11 attacks when he said, "Al Qaeda[2] is to terror what the Mafia is to crime." The comparison is instructive. During the great wave of immigration around the turn of the century, and for more than a generation after it was stopped in the 1920s, law enforcement had very little luck in penetrating the Mafia. This was because immigrants lived in enclaves with limited knowledge of English, were suspicious of government institutions, and clung to Old World prejudices and attitudes like "omerta" (the code of silence).

Assimilation vs. the Mafia. But with the end of mass immigration, the assimilation of Italian immigrants and their children accelerated and the offspring of the immigrants developed a sense of genuine membership and ownership in America—what John Fonte of the Hudson Institute calls "patriotic assimilation." It was this process that drained the waters within which the Mafia had been able to swim, allowing law enforcement to do its job more effectively, and eventually cripple the Mafia.

Anthropologist Francis Ianni described this process 30 years ago: "An era of Italo-American crime seems to be passing in large measure due to the changing character of the Italo-American community," including "the disappearance of the kinship model on which such [Mafia] families are based."

"After three generations of acculturation," Ianni continued, "this

2. Al-Qaeda is the terrorist network responsible for the September 11 attacks.

powerful pattern of organization is finally losing its hold on Italo-Americans generally—and on the crime families as well." In the same way, accelerating assimilation in Muslim immigrant communities by reducing immigration will make it harder for terrorists to operate there—harder to find cover, harder to recruit sympathizers, harder to raise funds.

Blending in. That this is a problem in Muslim immigrant communities is beyond dispute. A *New York Times* reporter wrote shortly after the attacks that there are many reasons that Islamic terrorists use Germany as a base, "among them the fact that the terrorists could blend into a society with a large Muslim population and more foreigners than any other in Europe."

This also applies in our own country. Another *Times* story observed about Paterson, N.J., that "The hijackers' stay here also shows how, in an area that speaks many languages and keeps absorbing immigrants, a few young men with no apparent means of support and no furniture can settle in for months without drawing attention."

Even worse than the role immigrant enclaves play in simply shielding terrorists is their role in recruiting new ones.

Nor is the role of the immigrant community entirely passive. Two of the 9/11 hijackers—Nawaf Alhamzi and Khalid Almihdhar—had been embraced by the Muslim immigrant community in San Diego. As *The Washington Post* noted, "From their arrival here in late 1999 until they departed a few months before the 9/11 attacks, Alhazmi and Almihdhar repeatedly enlisted help from San Diego's mosques and established members of its Islamic community. The terrorists leaned on them to find housing, open a bank account, obtain car insurance—even, at one point, get a job."

Recruiting terrorists. And even worse than the role immigrant enclaves play in simply shielding terrorists is their role in recruiting new ones. The *San Francisco Chronicle* reported on naturalized U.S. citizen Khalid Abu al Dahab, described as "a one-man communications hub" for al Qaeda, shuttling money and fake passports to terrorists around the world from his Silicon Valley apartment. According to the *Chronicle*, "Dahab said [terrorist Osama] bin Laden was eager to recruit American citizens of Middle Eastern descent." When Dahab and fellow terrorist and naturalized citizen Ali Mohammed (a U.S. army veteran and author of al Qaeda's terrorist handbook) traveled to Afghanistan in the mid-1990s to report on their efforts to recruit American citizens, "bin Laden praised their efforts and emphasized the necessity of recruiting as many Muslims with American citizenship as possible into the organization."

Perhaps the most disturbing example so far of such recruitment in immigrant communities comes from Lackawanna, N.Y., where six Yemeni Americans—five of them born and raised in the United States to immigrants parents—were arrested in September [2002] for operating an al Qaeda terrorist sleeper cell. The alleged ringleader of the cell, also born in the United States, is believed to be hiding in Yemen. The six arrested men are accused of traveling to Pakistan last year ostensibly for religious training and then going to an al Qaeda terrorist training camp in Afghanistan. The community that bred this cell is intimately shaped by ongoing immigration. As the *Buffalo News* put it:

> This is a piece of ethnic America where the Arabic-speaking Al-Jazeera television station is beamed in from Qatar through satellite dishes to Yemenite-American homes; where young children answer "Salaam" when the cell phone rings, while older children travel to the Middle East to meet their future husband or wife; where soccer moms don't seem to exist, and where girls don't get to play soccer—or, as some would say, football.

From 1991 through 2000, more than 16,000 Yemenis immigrated legally to the United States. In Lackawanna itself, the Arab population has ballooned by 175 percent during the 1990s. The median household income in the Yemeni neighborhood is 20 percent lower than in Lackawanna as a whole.

More immigrants, more cells. Nor is this likely to be the last such cell uncovered. As another story in *The Buffalo News* reported: "Federal officials say privately that there could be dozens of similar cells across the country, together posing a grave danger to national security. They believe that such cells tend to be concentrated in communities with large Arab populations, such as Detroit."

Yemen is not the only Middle Eastern country sending large numbers of immigrants. A recent Center for Immigration Studies report found that Middle Easterners are one of the fastest-growing immigrant groups in the United States, growing seven-fold since 1970, from fewer than 200,000 in 1970 to nearly 1.5 million in 2000. Assuming no change in our immigration policy, 1.1 million new immigrants (legal and illegal) from the Middle East are projected to settle here by 2010, and the total Middle Eastern immigrant population will grow to about 2.5 million. And that does not include the 570,000 U.S.-born children (under 18) who have at least one parent born in the Middle East, a number expected to grow to 950,000 by 2010.

What's more, the religious composition of Middle Eastern immigration has changed dramatically over the past thirty years. In 1970, an estimated 15 percent of immigrants from the region were Muslim, a mere 29,000 people; the rest were mostly Christians from Lebanon or Christian ethnic minorities such as Armenians fleeing predominately Muslim countries. By 2000, an estimated 73 percent of all Middle Eastern immigrants (1.1 million people) were Muslim.

Our response . . . can only be to cut immigration across the board.

Terrorists vs. Gangsters. Of course, Muslim immigrant communities are not alone in exhibiting characteristics that shield or even incubate criminality. For instance, as criminologist Ko-lin Chin has written, "The isolation of the Chinese community, the inability of American law enforcement authorities to penetrate the Chinese criminal underworld, and the reluctance of Chinese victims to come forward for help all conspire to enable Chinese gangs to endure." And the solution is the same for these other ethnic groups, as well; William Kleinknecht, author of *The New Ethnic Mobs*, notes that "If the mass immigration of Chinese should come to a halt, the Chinese gangster may disappear in a blaze of assimilation after a couple of decades."

While such criminality is certainly a cost of immigration that cannot be ignored, on its own it is not an adequate rationale to curb immigration. But the threat to our society posed by Middle Eastern terrorism is qualitatively different from the threat of the Mafia or Irish gangs in the past, or Russian, Chinese and Jamaican criminal organizations today. The danger from other immigrant groups' pimps, drug dealers, and small-scale killers pales in comparison to the effects of mass-casualty terrorism carried out by Muslim extremists.

Keep out the Arabs?

One solution could be simply to bar all immigrants and tourists from Muslim countries. A recent poll sponsored by the Chicago Council on Foreign Relations and the German Marshall Fund of the United States found considerable support for this approach, favored by 79 percent of the public and by 40 percent of people described as leaders.

But there are two problems with this, one practical, the other ideological. The practical problem is that barring arrivals from Muslim countries would be of limited utility. While such a policy, if applied to all categories of overseas arrivals for an indefinite period, might slow the growth of Muslim immigrant communities, it would have no effect on the INS's overall workload and thus not address one of the major security issues surrounding high immigration.

"Muslim extremists of non-Arabic appearance." What's more, targeting Muslim-majority countries wouldn't successfully screen out terrorists. As it is, applicants from Middle Eastern countries formally listed as sponsors of terrorism (Iran, Iraq, Libya, Sudan, Syria) have long faced a higher bar to entry—so instead, the 9/11 terrorists came from Muslim countries *not* on the official list of terrorist-sponsoring countries. Now that we are focusing more scrutiny on most Muslim-majority countries, we are likely to see terrorists coming from non-Muslim countries with large and radicalized Muslim minorities—the Philippines, India, China, Russia.

In fact, the FBI in September [2002] warned of just such a development with regard to Russian citizens. Because of increased scrutiny of visitors from Muslim nations, al Qaeda is said to have discussed "hijacking a commercial airliner using Muslim extremists of non-Arabic appearance," specifically "Chechen Muslims affiliated with al Qaeda, but already present in the United States."

In the unlikely event we were to bar everyone from Russia, the Philippines, etc., then the terrorists would almost certainly make greater use of Muslim citizens of western Europe and Canada . . .—and this is especially problematic, since visas are not currently required for citizens of these countries. As it happens, since the 9/11 attacks, dozens of people holding citizenship in Germany, Spain, France, Britain, and other European countries have been arrested for involvement in al Qaeda terrorist cells.

National-origins throwback. The impossibility of excluding radical Muslim terrorists by barring citizens of specific countries would force someone pursuing this approach to consider a religious test for immigration, which is clearly absurd. And that points to the second objection to an immigration policy targeting Muslims, an objection based on principle; special exclusions for Muslim immigrants, even if they were possible, would be a throwback to the national-origin quotas of the 1920s, the elimination of which was the only positive aspect of the hapless 1965 immigration-law changes.

Focusing on Muslims is certainly sensible as triage, as a way to decide where to start enforcing the law, as the Justice Department is doing by tackling the pool of 300,000-plus deportation absconders by starting with the 6,000 or so from the Middle East. But constructing a long term, Muslim-specific immigration policy would be contrary to American principles and politically unsustainable. After all, we have effectively been at war with Iraq for more than a decade and yet gave green cards to more than 40,000 Iraqis from 1991–2000—and not a single member of Congress has even suggested that we do otherwise.

Cut across the board. Our response, then, can only be to cut immigration across the board, regardless of the religion the immigrant claims to profess. Fortunately, such a policy change would serve other important national interests as well. It has been clear for some time that current immigration policy is an anachronism, on balance doing harm to the economy, the public fisc, national cohesion, and environmental quality.

Furthermore, there is enormous public support for such a reform. The aforementioned poll sponsored by the Chicago Council on Foreign Relations and the German Marshall Fund of the U.S. found that the majority of Americans supported reductions in immigration and fully 70 percent thought that reducing illegal immigration should be a very important goal of U.S. foreign policy. The same poll found an enormous gap between the public and opinion leaders on the immigration issue, with the public three times more likely to support reductions in immigration and four times more likely to see the level of immigration as a critical threat to U.S. interests. This would suggest that there is a significant opportunity awaiting the first politician who successfully harnesses these concerns.

The September 11 terrorist attacks have made immigration reform a matter of life and death. Cuts in both permanent and temporary immigration would contribute significantly to improved security by permitting more efficient management and by denying terrorists cover. We fail to act at our peril.

14

Homeland Security Measures Targeting Immigrants Are Unfair and Unnecessary

National Immigration Forum

The National Immigration Forum advocates and builds public support for public policies that welcome immigrants and refugees and that are fair and supportive to them.

Since September 11, the federal government has, in the name of homeland security, investigated, detained, and deported huge numbers of immigrants. The shifting of immigration functions from the Immigration and Naturalization Service to the Department of Homeland Security is a powerful signal that the government views all immigrants as potential terrorists and is moving away from the ideal of America as a nation that welcomes newcomers. Instead of threatening and harassing immigrants, the government should be working on gaining their trust and on building intelligence networks within immigrant communities in order to identify the very few immigrants that present a terrorist threat.

"Immigration is not a problem to be solved. It is the sign of a confident and successful nation. And people who seek to make America their home should be met in that spirit by representatives of our government. New arrivals should be greeted not with suspicion and resentment, but with openness and courtesy."

President George W. Bush
July 10, 2001
Ellis Island, New York

S ince the terrorist attacks of September 11, 2001, our government has struggled to respond so that Americans will be protected from further attacks. Legislation has been passed, agreements have been signed with neighbors and allies, government agencies have retooled for a new mission—all with the aim of making our nation less vulnerable to terrorism.

Unfortunately, thus far the government's response to terrorism has been somewhat schizophrenic. Rational, targeted measures meant to sift out the few who come here to do us harm from the millions of foreign-born who come here for legitimate reasons are being overshadowed by actions that have cast a wide net, hauling in hundreds of innocent persons and creating an atmosphere of fear in immigrant communities. The scattershot edicts from the Attorney General [John Ashcroft], for example, actually work at cross purposes with the more targeted efforts needed to keep us safe, creating a perception in immigrant communities that *any* contact with the government—even for those who now have resident status—might lead to their arrest and permanent exile from their adopted country.

The need for better intelligence

The Key to Success in Fighting Terrorism: Intelligence. The key to fighting terrorism effectively is intelligence. We must learn who has plans to harm us, and that information must be shared with the agencies that serve as gatekeepers to our country. To do a better job, we must cooperate with intelligence agencies around the world that are collecting information on known or potential terrorists. We must disrupt their criminal and financial networks, and cripple their operations. In addition, we must have reliable travel documents that will identify persons entering the U.S. We also must work with our neighbors, Mexico and Canada, so that anyone trying to enter the North American continent will be screened in a similar way.

Here is where we have had a measure of success: new legislation, such as the Enhanced Border Security and Visa Entry Reform Act, has given the government new tools to gather intelligence and identify potential terrorists, and to make sure that our gatekeeper agencies—the Immigration and Naturalization Service (INS) and the State Department—have the information they need to keep terrorists out. The Bush Administration has signed "Smart Border" agreements with Canada and Mexico, to prevent terrorists from using those countries as staging grounds for attacks on the U.S.

Policy Reform: Building Trust in Immigrant Communities. There are things the government could do that would greatly assist its ability to collect intelligence within the U.S. Using the increasingly popular tactic of community policing, police departments across the country could redouble their efforts to build trust in immigrant communities. By establishing good relations with communities of the foreign born, the police will be in a better position to collect useful bits of intelligence that might prevent future acts of terrorism. An overhaul of our immigration laws would also increase opportunities to gain intelligence on those already inside the U.S. Providing opportunities for undocumented immigrants to step out of the shadows and gain legal status, in exchange for making themselves known, would significantly shrink the haystack within which the needle of terrorism hides. The best way to enforce the laws is to create laws that are enforceable. Congress should reform our immigration laws to provide more legal channels for immigrants coming to work or join family members, so that they can be subjected to background checks and given legal visas if they qualify. Then, our enforcement agencies could shift their efforts away from keeping workers away from employers and focus instead on keeping out terrorists.

On this score, government actions have hindered, rather than helped, the fight against terrorism. Rather than complete the promising discussions on immigration reform begun with Mexico prior to September 11, the Administration and Congress have put immigration reform on the back burner. Instead of reforming our immigration laws to reward otherwise law-abiding workers who are desperate for more opportunities to work here legally, the government seems to have come under the influence of those who would treat all immigrants as terrorists. The cumulative effect of a series of government actions at all levels has created a siege atmosphere in immigrant communities, particularly those of Middle Eastern descent. For example, the Justice Department has made vague pronouncements giving all police the authority to enforce immigration laws. Letters sent by the Social Security Administration to employers have pushed hundreds of thousands of immigrant workers from their jobs into the underground economy. States are making it more difficult for some immigrants to drive legally. The Supreme Court has ruled that immigrant workers without proper papers cannot expect justice if they are illegally fired by their employers. The Justice Department has announced it will enforce an obscure 50-year-old law turning immigrants into criminals if they have not notified the government of a change of address.

Instead of looking for the needle in the haystack, the government has added bale after bale of hay to that haystack. If the goal is finding and rooting out potential terrorists among us, many of the initiatives launched in recent months can only be counterproductive. The remainder of this backgrounder summarizes some recent actions of the government—the Department of Justice in particular—which, taken together, constitute a backlash against all immigrants and refugees.

America's heritage as a nation of immigrants

There have been a series of actions taken by the Administration, Congress, the courts, and the states that, though they may have nothing to do with the fight against terrorism, have occurred during the past year and have acted to push immigrants outside the circle instead of drawing them in.

Immigration Through the Lens of Anti-Terrorism. Congress and the Bush Administration have created a Department of Homeland Security, a new federal agency dedicated to fighting and preventing terrorism. The entire immigration function of the government will be contained within the new department. This reorganization is a powerful signal that all immigrants will now be viewed as terrorist threats.

Simply burying what is now the INS—an agency that seems at times to be nearly paralyzed with dysfunction—in a mega-bureaucracy with an anti-terrorist mission will not increase our security. Rather, the immigration function must be re-organized so that it can both effectively contribute to the homeland security mission *and* process the applications of immigrants and visitors in a timely manner. There has been much thinking on how to reorganize the agency so that it may accomplish its dual enforcement and service missions by separating service and enforcement chains of command, and having an executive with clout to coordinate the separate functions and to elevate the immigration function within the federal bureaucracy. Unfortunately, the law that created the Department of Homeland Security failed to take into account that thinking.

No Match for Reality. The Social Security Administration has sent out more than 750,000 letters to employers, telling them that a Social Security number they have supplied does not match one in its database. Thousands of immigrants are losing their jobs, driving them from jobs where they were paying taxes into work in the underground economy. Perhaps more than anything, this example illustrates the disconnect between our immigration laws and the reality of our economy—that there are not sufficient legal opportunities for immigrants to work for employers who are in need of their labor.

The Department of Justice has launched a number of initiatives since September 11 that, taken together, cast a wide net that threatens to entangle millions of America's newcomers.

Driving the Wrong Way. Since September 11, states across the country are making it more difficult for immigrants to obtain drivers licenses—ostensibly to make the document more secure. These states are in effect changing the purpose of a license, from a document used to show that the operator of a motor vehicle understands the rules of the road and is licensed to drive, into a kind of internal passport. With the option to drive legally closed to them, some immigrants who want to obey the law may be forced for job-related reasons to drive without a license—and without insurance. The practical result of making it more difficult for immigrants to get licenses, then, is to make the roads less safe for all of us.

Mass Firing of Baggage Screeners. After September 11, Congress passed a law requiring all airport baggage screeners to be U.S. citizens. Thousands of immigrants who have not yet become citizens have been fired from jobs they have been trained for and often held for many years. In their place, airports have had to hire citizens who have to be trained anew. Ironically, non-citizens can serve in the military and the National Guard, where they may watch over the citizen baggage screeners.

Work Without Pay. In March, the Supreme Court handed down a decision which, in effect, gives employers who use undocumented workers the green light to fire their workers as soon as they begin to stick up for their rights in the workplace. In a decision known as *Hoffman Plastics*, the court said that the worker was not entitled to back pay—a common remedy when workers are fired illegally—from the time they were illegally fired. Some unscrupulous employers are taking this as an opportunity to not pay some of their workers even for the time they have worked. As other government actions make it harder for some immigrants to work for well-intentioned employers, they will to a greater extent be relegated to jobs with unscrupulous employers trying to test the limits of our labor laws.

Red Tape for the Persecuted. The events of September 11 seem to have shaken America's leadership in protecting the world's persecuted. Our refugee resettlement program slowed to a trickle as refugees, already the most diligently-screened category of immigrants admitted to this country, became subject to additional security screening. In Fiscal Year 2002, the U.S. took in 27,113 refugees—less than half of the 70,000 target for that year. Add to this the Bush Administration's lower ceiling for allocated refugee admissions in Fiscal Year 2003, and it is apparent that the United States is reducing its commitment to protect the world's most vulnerable people.

Immigration Reform Goes to the Back Burner. Prior to September 11, immigrant communities had high hopes that our government would fix our broken immigration system. Presidents [George W.] Bush and Vicente Fox of Mexico were in negotiations that could have led to a "grand bargain" on immigration, including legalizing the status of hard-working immigrants who have been living in this country for a number of years, and expanding opportunities for more people to come to the U.S. legally in the future. Although the Administration has said repeatedly that it wants to get back to that positive agenda, there has been very little action. In fact, since September 11, our border policy has continued to focus on keeping Mexican workers away from American employers, as more agents are deployed to the Southern border while the Northern border has received only token reinforcement. Our border policy has led to a record number of deaths of would-be immigrant workers trying to cross the border in remote desert terrain. Meanwhile, many of the internal enforcement measures the government has recently adopted are driving those working here without permission further underground.

Department of Justice actions

The Department of Justice has launched a number of initiatives since September 11 that, taken together, cast a wide net that threatens to entangle millions of America's newcomers. Even immigrants who have established themselves here have come to worry that they could be sent into permanent exile for the most minor offense—or thrown into detention indefinitely without charge.

A Criminal Move. The Justice Department has given notice that it will start enforcing a little-used, 50-year-old law making it a crime for an immigrant not to report a change of address to the INS within ten days of moving. The law also permits the government to send people into permanent exile if they fail to send in their change of address form. The problem is, millions of non-citizens (including perhaps as many as nine million legal permanent residents) who have moved since they were last in communication with the INS did not know about this rule. Potentially, they could all be facing criminal charges, and they are all at risk of deportation. This decision gives the Justice Department the option to pick up just about anyone. If the Department follows its own precedent in other initiatives since September 11, a decision to punish someone for not filing an address change form will depend on whether the person is Arab or Muslim. As if to illustrate this suspicion, the first person to face deportation for failing to file a change of address form was a Palestinian man. (A judge threw the case out.)

Those who do know about this obscure law, and follow the rules, may not fare any better. The INS has not been able to process the forms that have been mailed in. In July 2002, the INS had 200,000 change of address forms sitting in boxes in an underground storage facility. That was before the Justice Department announced it would strictly enforce the law. In the three months after the announcement, the INS received 700,000 additional forms that are now also sitting in boxes, in storage. Some of the people who filled out the forms now sitting in those boxes could be deported or held on criminal charges because the INS has not entered their change of address into a computer, and they would be unable to prove that they had indeed followed the rules.

"The policy of 'shaking the trees' in Islamic communities . . . alienates the very people on whom law enforcement depends for leads and may turn out to be counterproductive."

APB for Foreigners. In April 2002, press reports revealed that the Justice Department would reverse a long-standing government policy which logically kept responsibility for enforcing civil immigration law with trained officers of the Immigration and Naturalization Service. In the switch, the Department was declaring that local and state police agencies had the "inherent authority" to enforce immigration laws. Millions may be affected by this rule as law enforcement officers, untrained in immigration law, stop and question foreigners and other Americans who look or sound like they might be foreign.

Most big-city police agencies have already rejected this authority. They know that their ability to fight real crime depends on building trust in their communities, and if immigrants fear being turned over to the INS, they will not turn to the police if they have been a victim or witness a crime—or if they have information that might be useful in deterring future terrorism. As Montgomery County, Maryland Police Chief Charles Moose said, "[T]his movement by the federal government to say that they want local officers to become INS agents is against the core values of community policing: partnerships, assisting people, and being there to solve problems. . . . I think it would be totally inappropriate to go down that path." The point was dramatically illustrated in Chief Moose's own jurisdiction, when police struggled to overcome the reluctance of immigrants to step forward as potential witnesses in the famous Washington sniper case.

Your Papers, Please. In September 2002, the Justice Department began implementing a tracking scheme that requires visitors from certain countries—and others who an immigration inspector decides meet certain secret criteria—to register with the government by providing their fingerprints, photographs and other information when they enter the country. After thirty days, they have to appear again to register, and then at one year intervals after that. The scheme was expanded twice in November 2002 to cover certain individuals from 18 mostly Middle-Eastern countries who had already entered the U.S. prior to September 10th or 30th of 2002. It was again expanded in December, to cover individuals from an additional two countries. Already, this program has resulted in chaos at ports of entry, data overload for the INS, and foreign governments scrambling for "exemptions" from these bureaucratic and empty requirements.

Round Up the Usual Suspects. The Justice Department's actions have hit American Muslims and Arab Americans the hardest. In its round-up of immigrants as part of the post-September 11 investigation, the Justice Department has taken into custody hundreds of men with Middle Eastern and Arabic backgrounds. At the end of 2001, the Justice Department announced that it would track down and interview 5,000 Arabs in the U.S. They were interviewed not because they were suspected of having a connection to terrorism, but because they were Arab, in a certain age range, and were newly arrived in the U.S. Out of the 5,000, twenty were taken into custody, mostly on immigration charges. In the spring of 2002, another 3,000 interviews were ordered.

In each of its enforcement initiatives since September 11, the Department has made it a point to enforce the law first on immigrants of Middle Eastern descent. For example, an effort to track down 300,000 immigrants who have been given final deportation orders has focused first on Middle Eastern men. Former CIA counterterrorism head Vincent Cannistraro noted that the Justice Department's "detention of thousands of immigrant Muslims—the policy of 'shaking the trees' in Islamic communities—alienates the very people on whom law enforcement depends for leads and may turn out to be counterproductive."

Secret Trials. Shortly after September 11, the Justice Department's chief immigration judge issued instructions to hundreds of immigration judges to close to the public all immigration-related trials of individuals picked up in connection with the September 11 investigations. The order has applied to more that 600 "special interest" immigration cases. Not only is the courtroom closed to visitors, family, and the press, but the restriction extends to even "confirming or denying whether such a case is on the docket." Because they are being held in secret, there is no way to determine if these trials are being conducted fairly, or if immigrants are being given proper due process as the government tries to deport them.

Will the broad attacks launched by the government on the rights and liberties of immigrants in this country make us safer? It is hard to see how.

The Disappeared. Since September 11, hundreds of immigrants have been thrown in prison without being told why, without access to a lawyer, without anyone on the outside—including their families—knowing where they are being held. Most of those in secret detention are officially being held for minor immigration violations. Some, even after they stop fighting the government's efforts to deport them, are still held for months with no reason given. Former Secretary of State Warren Christopher said that this tactic—of snatching people in the middle of the night and secretly jailing them—reminded him of the "disappeareds" in Argentina. "I'll never forget going to Argentina and seeing the mothers marching in the streets asking for the names of those being held by the government," Mr. Christopher said. "We must be careful in this country about taking people into custody without revealing their names."

Removal Expedited. In November of 2002, the INS announced that it was greatly expanding a procedure called expedited removal. This procedure gives low-level immigration officers the power to immediately remove from the U.S. anyone who does not have proper travel documents. Up to then, the procedure had been used only as people tried to enter the U.S. at ports of entry. The expansion of expedited removal applies to all persons arriving by sea, if an immigration officer had not admitted them. Even persons living and working in this country for up to two years (and perhaps longer) will be subject to this treatment. Justified in part on national security grounds, the new expedited removal powers will be primarily focused not on terrorists, but on poor Haitians fleeing economic and political turmoil in Haiti.

Benefit in Doubt. Applicants for immigration benefits—such as naturalization or lawful permanent residence—have always had to undergo security clearances, including an FBI background check. In May 2002, the INS suddenly started to require its adjudicators to start checking all applications on an additional system—the Interagency Border Inspection System—normally used at the border to check people entering the country. Many offices in the interior of the U.S. did not have access to this system. In other offices, INS personnel were not trained in its use. As a result, the backlogs for which the INS has become infamous are on the rise again. The backlogs may rise dramatically in the future, especially if the immigration function's move to the massive new Department of Homeland Security does not go smoothly. The larger bureaucracy's priority will be to keep out terrorists, and processing of immigration applications may slow to a trickle just as the refugee resettlement program has under a new security regime.

Preserve American ideals

Immigrants Want to Embrace America; Does America Want to Embrace Immigrants? Despite the government's efforts to make life difficult, immigrants are embracing America in near record numbers. By the end of the government's 2002 fiscal year, citizenship applications were near an all-time high, and up 40% over the year before. Many reacted to the attacks against America by showing their patriotism for their adopted country. At the same time, there is a feeling that only citizenship will protect them from the whims of a government that is making life in America more tenuous with each passing month.

For those unlucky enough not to be eligible for citizenship at this time, there is a constant fear of losing everything they have built up during years in the U.S. Even long-time permanent residents, who up to now may have been confident that they knew America and America knew them, are now wondering whether the government will find some other obscure law that could be used as an excuse to deport them.

Busywork Will Not Make Us Safer. Will the broad attacks launched by the government on the rights and liberties of immigrants in this country make us safer? It is hard to see how. The INS has been charged with, or is being required to place new priority on, collecting information such as change of address data from all immigrants, biographical and academic data from students, and entry and exit data from certain immigrants of "special concern." Assuming the INS can cope with the new workload, all of this extra information will keep data-enterers busy but will be difficult to analyze, because it will not tell the government which of the millions of immigrants from whom the information is collected may have harmful intent.

The government measures described here make it more difficult for millions of immigrants to work and provide for their families, and will drive those without permission to be here further underground—not a good thing if we would like to know who is here and what information they might have for us. Instead, we need to bring these people out of the shadows by moving forward with a legalization program that gives us a chance to scrutinize their backgrounds and determine whether or not they should remain in this country. We also need to open up legal avenues for workers to come in the future, to take the wind from the sails of the lucrative human smuggling business that thrives when so many are shut out from legal opportunities to come here. That industry could just as easily serve clients who come here to do us harm.

The government's policies towards immigrants have strayed far from the ideals mentioned by President Bush in his July 2001 speech quoted at the beginning of this viewpoint. It is time that we reverse course, stop blaming all immigrants for the actions of a handful of foreign-born terrorists, and focus on what really will make us safer from terrorism.

Organizations to Contact

The editors have compiled the following list of organizations concerned with the issues debated in this book. The descriptions are derived from materials provided by the organizations. All have publications or information available for interested readers. The list was compiled on the date of publication of the present volume; the information provided here may change. Be aware that many organizations take several weeks or longer to respond to inquiries, so allow as much time as possible.

American Civil Liberties Union (ACLU)
132 W. 43rd St., New York, NY 10036
(212) 944-9800 • fax: (212) 869-9065
e-mail: aclu@aclu.org • website: www.aclu.org

The ACLU is a national organization that defends Americans' civil rights guaranteed in the U.S. Constitution. It offers numerous reports, fact sheets, and policy statements on a wide variety of issues, including the right to privacy, church-state separation, and the government's antiterrorism efforts. It publishes and distributes policy statements, pamphlets, and reports, including *Civil Liberties After 9-11: The ACLU Defends Freedom* and *Bigger Monster, Weaker Chains: The Growth of an American Surveillance Society*.

American Enterprise Institute
1150 17th St. NW, Washington, DC 20036
(202) 862-5800 • fax: (202) 862-7177
website: www.aei.org

The American Enterprise Institute for Public Policy Research is a scholarly research institute that is dedicated to preserving limited government, private enterprise, and a strong foreign policy and national defense. It publishes books, including *Study of Revenge: The First World Trade Center Attack* and *Saddam Hussein's War Against America*. Articles about terrorism and homeland security can be found in its magazine, *American Enterprise*, and on its website.

ANSER Institute for Homeland Security
e-mail: homelandsecurity@anser.org • website: www.homelandsecurity.org

The institute is a nonprofit, nonpartisan think tank that works to educate the public about homeland security issues. The institute's website contains a virtual library of fact sheets, reports, legislation, and government documents and statistics on homeland security issues. It also publishes the *Journal of Homeland Security* and a weekly newsletter.

Arab American Institute (AAI)
1600 K St. NW, Suite 601, Washington, DC 20006
(202) 429-9210
website: www.aaiusa.org

The institute is a nonprofit organization committed to the civic and political empowerment of Americans of Arab descent. AAI opposes ethnic profiling

111

and the restriction of immigrants' civil liberties in the name of homeland security. AAI provides policy, research, and public affairs services to support a broad range of community activities. It publishes a quarterly newsletter called *Issues*, a weekly bulletin called *Countdown*, and the report *Healing the Nation: The Arab American Experience After September 11*.

Brookings Institution
1775 Massachusetts Ave. NW, Washington, DC 20036
(202) 797-6000 • fax: (202) 797-6004
e-mail: brookinfo@brook.edu • website: www.brookings.org

The institution is a think tank that conducts research and education in foreign policy, economics, government, and the social sciences. In 2001 it began America's Response to Terrorism, a project that provides briefings and analysis to the public and which is featured on the center's website. Other publications include the quarterly *Brookings Review*, periodic *Policy Briefs*, and reports including *Protecting the American Homeland: One Year On*.

Cato Institute
1000 Massachusetts Ave. NW, Washington, DC 20001-5403
(202) 842-0200 • fax: (202) 842-3490
e-mail: cato@cato.org • website: www.cato.org

The institute is a nonpartisan public policy research foundation dedicated to limiting the role of government and protecting individual liberties. It publishes the quarterly magazine *Regulation*, the bimonthly *Cato Policy Report*, and numerous policy papers and articles. Works on homeland security include "Breaking the Vicious Cycle: Preserving Our Liberties While Fighting Terrorism," and "How Should the U.S. Respond to Terrorism?"

Center for Constitutional Rights (CCR)
666 Broadway, 7th Floor, New York, NY 10012
(212) 614-6464 • fax: (212) 614-6499
website: www.ccr-ny.org

CCR is a nonprofit legal and educational organization dedicated to protecting and advancing the rights guaranteed by the U.S. Constitution and the Universal Declaration of Human Rights. CCR uses litigation to empower minority and poor communities and to strengthen the broader movement for constitutional and human rights. The organization opposes the government's curtailment of civil liberties since the September 11, 2001, terrorist attacks. CCR publishes books, pamphlets, facts sheets, and reports, such as *The State of Civil Liberties: One Year Later*.

Center for Democracy and Technology (CDT)
1634 Eye St. NW, Suite 1100, Washington, DC 20006
(202) 637-9800
website: www.cdt.org

CDT's mission is to develop public policy solutions that advance constitutional civil liberties and democratic values in the new computer and communications media. With regard to homeland security, CDT maintains that surrendering freedom will not purchase security and that open communications networks are a positive force in the fight against violence and intolerance. It opposes measures to increase government surveillance, such as in some of the provisions of the USA PATRIOT Act. The CDT website provides numerous fact sheets and news updates on government electronic surveillance, wiretapping, and cybersecurity.

Center for Immigration Studies
1522 K St. NW, Suite 820, Washington, DC 20005-1202
(202) 466-8185 • fax: (202) 466-8076
e-mail: center@cis.org • website: www.cis.org

The Center for Immigration Studies is a think tank dedicated to research and analysis of the economic, social, and demographic impacts of immigration on the United States. An independent, non-profit, research organization, the center aims to expand public support for an immigration policy that is both pro-immigrant and low-immigration. It believes that restricting immigration should be a top priority in the government's homeland security strategy. Among its publications are the papers "Visas for Terrorists: What Went Wrong?," "The Open Door: How Militant Islamic Terrorists Entered and Remained in the United States, 1993–2001," and "The USA PATRIOT Act of 2001: A Summary of the Anti-Terrorism Law's Immigration-Related Provisions."

Central Intelligence Agency (CIA)
Office of Public Affairs, Washington, DC 20505
(703) 482-0623 • fax: (703) 482-1739
website: www.cia.gov

The CIA was created in 1947 with the signing of the National Security Act (NSA) by President Harry S. Truman. The NSA charged the Director of Central Intelligence (DCI) with coordinating the nation's intelligence activities and correlating, evaluating, and disseminating intelligence that affects national security. The CIA is an independent agency, responsible to the president through the DCI, and accountable to the American people through the Intelligence Oversight Committee of the U.S. Congress. Publications, including the *National Strategy for Combating Terrorism* and *Factbook on Intelligence*, are available on its website.

Department of Homeland Security
Washington, DC 20528
website: www.dhs.gov

The creation of the DHS in March 2003 is the most significant transformation of the U.S. government since 1947, when President Harry S. Truman merged the various branches of the U.S. armed forces into the Department of Defense to better coordinate the nation's defense against military threats. In a similar vein DHS merges twenty-two previously disparate domestic agencies into one department to protect the nation against threats to the homeland. DHS's priority is to protect the nation against terrorist attacks. Component agencies analyze threats and intelligence, guard America's borders and airports, protect critical infrastructure, and coordinate the U.S. response to future emergencies. The DHS website offers a wide variety of information on homeland security, including press releases, speeches and testimony, and reports on topics such as airport security, weapons of mass destruction, planning for and responding to emergencies, the DHS threat advisory system, and border control.

Electronic Privacy Information Center (EPIC)
1718 Connecticut Ave. NW, Suite 200, Washington, DC 20009
(202) 483-1140
website: www.epic.org

EPIC is a public interest research center that works to focus public attention on emerging civil liberties issues and to protect privacy, the First Amendment, and constitutional values. It supports privacy-protection legislation and provides information on how individuals can protect their online privacy. EPIC publishes the *EPIC Alert* newsletter and the *Privacy Law Sourcebook* as well as the report *Your Papers, Please: From the State Drivers License to a National Identification System.*

Federal Bureau of Investigation (FBI)
935 Pennsylvania Ave. NW, Room 7972, Washington, DC 20535
(202) 324-3000
website: www.fbi.gov

The FBI is the principle investigative arm of the U.S. Department of Justice. Its mission is to uphold the law through the investigation of violations of federal criminal law; to protect the United States from foreign intelligence and terrorist activities; to provide leadership and law enforcement assistance to federal, state, local, and international agencies; and to perform these responsibilities in a manner that is responsive to the needs of the public and is faithful to the Constitution of the United States. Press releases, congressional statements, speeches, and information on the war on terrorism and the FBI's most wanted terrorists, are available on the agency's website.

Heritage Foundation
214 Massachusetts Ave. NE, Washington, DC 20002-4999
(202) 546-4400
website: www.heritage.org

The Heritage Foundation is a research and educational institute—a think tank—whose mission is to formulate and promote conservative public policies based on the principles of free enterprise, limited government, individual freedom, traditional American values, and a strong national defense. Heritage research and analysis on homeland security issues include the papers "Principles for Safeguarding Civil Liberties in an Age of Terrorism," "Congress Should Not Prematurely Short-Circuit the Total Information Awareness Program," and "Improving Efficiency and Reducing Costs in the Department of Homeland Security."

Independence Institute
14142 Denver West Parkway, Suite 185, Golden, CO 80401
(303) 279-6536
website: www.i2i.org

The institute is established upon the eternal truths of the Declaration of Independence. It is a nonpartisan, nonprofit public policy research organization dedicated to providing timely information to concerned citizens, government officials, and public opinion leaders. It emphasizes private-sector and community-based solutions to social issues. Institute papers on homeland security include "The Expanding Surveillance State: Facial Recognition" and "Just Say No to National I.D. Cards."

National Immigration Forum (NIF)
220 I St. NE, Suite 220, Washington, DC 20002-4362
(202) 544-0004
website: www.immigrationforum.org

The purpose of the NIF is to embrace and uphold America's tradition as a nation of immigrants. The forum advocates and builds public support for public policies that welcome immigrants and refugees and that are fair and supportive to newcomers to the United States. The NIF website offers a special section on immigration in the wake of the September 11, 2001, terrorist attacks which includes the report *Immigrants in the Crosshairs: Diverse Voices Speak Out Against the Backlash* and *The Way Forward on Immigration Policy.*

National Security Agency
9800 Savage Rd., Ft. Meade, MD 20755-6248
(301) 688-6524
website: www.nsa.gov

The National Security Agency coordinates, directs, and performs activities such as designing cipher systems, which protect American information systems and produce foreign intelligence information. It is the largest employer of mathematicians in the United States and also hires the nation's best codemakers and codebreakers. Speeches, briefings, and reports are available on the website.

Bibliography

Books

Kurt M. Campbell and Michele A. Flourney — *To Prevail: An American Strategy for the Campaign Against Terrorism.* Washington, DC: Center for Strategic and International Studies, 2001.

Nancy Chang et al. — *Silencing Political Dissent: How Post–September 11 Anti-Terrorism Measures Threaten Our Civil Liberties.* New York: Seven Stories Press, 2002.

David Cole and James X. Dempsey — *Terrorism and the Constitution: Sacrificing Civil Liberties in the Name of National Security.* New York: New Press, 2002.

Anthony H. Cordesman — *Terrorism, Asymmetric Warfare, and Weapons of Mass Destruction: Defending the U.S. Homeland.* Westport, CT: Praeger, 2002.

Lynn E. Davis — *Organizing for Homeland Security.* Santa Monica, CA: Rand, 2002.

Alan M. Dershowitz — *Shouting Fire: Civil Liberties in a Turbulent Age.* Boston: Little, Brown, 2002.

Kathlyn Gay — *Silent Death: The Threat of Chemical and Biological Terrorism.* Brookfield, CT: Twenty-First Century Books, 2001.

Ted Gottfried — *Homeland Security vs. Constitutional Rights.* Brookfield, CT: Twenty-First Century Books, 2003.

Stanley Hauerwas and Frank Lentricchia, eds. — *Dissent from the Homeland: Essays After September 11.* Durham, NC: Duke University Press, 2002.

Katrina vanden Heuvel, ed. — *A Just Response: The* Nation *on Terrorism, Democracy, and September 11.* New York: Thunder's Mouth Press, 2002.

Michael A. Ledeen — *The War Against the Terror Masters.* New York: St. Martin's Press, 2002.

Michael E. O'Hanlon et al. — *Protecting the American Homeland: A Preliminary Analysis.* Washington, DC: Brookings Institution, 2002.

William H. Rehnquist — *All the Laws but One: Civil Liberties in Wartime.* New York: Knopf, 1998.

Phil Scraton, ed. — *Beyond September 11: An Anthology of Dissent.* London: Pluto Press, 2002.

Paul Wilkinson — *Terrorism Versus Democracy: The Liberal State Response.* London: Frank Cass, 2001.

Periodicals

Sonia Arrison and Solveig Singleton	"Symposium: Will the Government's Use of Biometrics Endanger American Civil Liberties?" *Insight on the News*, February 25, 2002.
David Carr	"The Futility of 'Homeland Defense,'" *Atlantic Monthly*, January 2002.
David Cole	"Enemy Aliens and American Freedoms: Experience Teaches Us That Whatever the Threat, Certain Principles Are Sacrosanct," *Nation*, September 23, 2002.
David Cole	"National Security State," *Nation*, December 17, 2001.
Robert Cottrol	"Homeland Security: Restoring Civic Virtue," *American Enterprise*, January/February 2003.
Valerie L. Demmer	"Civil Liberties and Homeland Security," *Humanist*, January/February 2002.
Ekaterina Drozdova and Michael Samoilov	"Security *and* Liberty: How to Protect the Nation Against Terrorism Without Sacrificing Our Civil Liberty," *Hoover Digest*, Winter 2002.
Katherine Eban	"Waiting for Bioterror: Is Our Public Health System Ready?" *Nation*, December 9, 2002.
Economist	"A Question of Freedom: Civil Liberties and Terrorism," March 8, 2003.
Economist	"Washington's Mega-Merger: The New Department of Homeland Security," November 23, 2002.
George P. Fletcher	"War and the Constitution: Bush's Military Tribunals Haven't Got a Leg to Stand On," *American Prospect*, January 1, 2002.
Nick Gillespie	"Freedom for Safety: An Old Trade—and a Useless One," *Reason*, October 2002.
Charles Krauthammer	"The Case for Profiling: Why Random Searches of Airline Travelers Are a Useless Charade," *Time*, March 18, 2002.
Richard Lowry	"Profiles of Cowardice: How to Deal with the Terrorist Threat—and How Not To," *National Review*, January 28, 2002.
Charles C. Mann	"Homeland Insecurity," *Atlantic Monthly*, September 2002.
Anna Mulrine and Nancy Bentrup	"The Power of Secrets," *U.S. News & World Report*, January 27, 2003.
Kate O'Beirne	"The DHS Debacle: A Department We'll Spend a Lifetime Criticizing," *National Review*, August 12, 2002.
Richard A. Posner	"Security Versus Civil Liberties," *Atlantic Monthly*, December 2001.
Romesh Ratnesar	"The State of Our Defense," *Time*, February 24, 2003.

118   *At Issue*

Anthony D. Romero   "In Defense of Liberty: Accountability and Responsiveness to Civil Liberties," *Vital Speeches of the Day*, January 1, 2002.

Jeffrey Rosen   "Security Check: How to Stop Big Brother," *New Republic*, December 16, 2001.

William Safire   "You Are a Suspect," *New York Times*, November 14, 2002.

Peter H. Schuck   "A Case for Profiling," *American Lawyer*, January 2002.

Bruce Shapiro   "All in the Name of Security: The Administration Is Using September 11 to Curtail Our Civil Liberties," *Nation*, October 22, 2001.

Lamar Smith and Angelo M. Codevilla   "Symposium: Are Expanded Police Powers Needed to Ensure U.S. Security?" *Insight on the News*, October 22, 2001.

Abraham D. Sofaer and Paul R. Williams   "Doing Justice During Wartime: Why Military Tribunals Make Sense," *Policy Review*, February 2002.

Gene Stephens   "Can We Be Both Safe and Free?: The Dilemma Terrorism Creates," *USA Today*, January 2003.

Stuart Taylor Jr.   "How Civil-Libertarian Hysteria May Endanger Us All," *National Journal*, February 22, 2003.

William Thornberry and Eric R. Taylor   "Symposium: Is a New Federal Agency Needed to Defend Against Terrorist Attacks?" *Insight on the News*, March 26, 2001.

Fareed Zakaria   "Freedom vs. Security: Delicate Balance: The Case for 'Smart Profiling' as a Weapon in the War on Terror," *Newsweek*, July 8, 2002.

Index

affirmative action, 87–88
Afghanistan, 15
Agre, Philip, 82
airport security, 16
  baggage screeners and, 9, 105
  facial recognition technology for,
    73–77, 79, 80
  racial profiling and, 86–88
Alhazmi, Nawaq, 69, 98
Almidhar, Khalid, 69, 98
American Civil Liberties Union (ACLU),
  13, 14, 81
Arab immigration. *See* immigration
Armey, Dick, 84
Ashcroft, John
  investigative tools requested by, 13–14
  preventive detention used by, 33
  view on dissenting opinions by, 15
Atick, Joseph, 73, 84
attorney-client communications, 19–20
attorney general
  power of, to detain suspects, 50–52
  see also Ashcroft, John

baggage screeners, 9, 105
Al Barakaat, 40
Bill of Rights, judiciary should uphold,
  52–53
Black, Hugo, 84
border control issues, 93–94, 103, 106
  see also immigration
Britain, use of facial recognition
  software in, 81–82
Bryant, Daniel J., 45
Burnham, David, 28
Bush, George W., 54, 97, 106
Butterfield, Jeanne, 94

Cannistraro, Vincent, 108
Chang, Nancy, 43
checks and balances, threat to, 18–19
Cheney, Dick, 18
Chin, Ko-lin, 99
Chinese immigrant community, 99–100
Christopher, Warren, 108–109
Church Committee, 50
CIA dossiers, 16
citizen status, as indicator of terrorist
  involvement, 17–18
civil liberties
  homeland security measures and

infringements on, 9, 11–12
  should not be restricted to protect,
    23–33
  undermine, 13–22
  USA PATRIOT Act has undermined,
    43–53
  vigilance is needed to protect, 21–22
Colatosti, Tom, 80
Cole, David, 12, 20, 89
Congress
  passage of USA PATRIOT Act by, 43–44
  USA PATRIOT Act undermines, 18–19
courts. *See* judiciary branch
criminal law, USA PATRIOT Act
  strengthens, 39

Dahab, Khalid Abu al, 98
Debs, Eugene, 52
Defense Advanced Research Projects
  Agency, 68
Dempsey, James X., 89
Denver Police Intelligence Unit, 83–84
Department of Homeland Security
  (DHS)
  creation of, 10
  duties of, 56–57
  immigration and, 104–105
  insufficient authority of, 59–60
  may make Americans less safe, 58–64
  will not facilitate information sharing,
    63–64
  will protect against terrorists, 54–57
Dershowitz, Alan, 32
detainment
  of immigrants after September 11,
    14–16, 18–20, 44, 108–109
  of immigrants, violated constitutional
    protections, 50–52
  rule of law and, 20
  secrecy surrounding, 20

electronic surveillance. *See* surveillance
enemy combatants, 21, 32–33
England, Gordon, 56
Enhanced Border Security and Visa
  Entry Reform Act, 103
equality, threat to, 17–18
Equal Protection Clause, 90
ethnic profiling. *See* racial profiling
executive branch
  new powers given to, 44–45

119